CARNIVAL KNOWLEDGE

GENE SORROWS

SUN PUBLISHING

ACKNOWLEDGEMENTS

To list everyone who has helped in my efforts would be impossible, for the list grows daily, but to the ones who have given of their time and energies I not only commend you for your personal sacrifice but even more for the tremendous courage displayed against an overwhelming adversary.

THANK YOU – Carl Shoffler, Lt. Tony Morris and his whole squad, Tom Heffernan, Jerry Matheson, Prior Price, Phil Harker, Bill Howard, Brad Pope, and many others.

Copyright © 1983
All rights reserved.

THIS BOOK MAY NOT BE REPRODUCED IN WHOLE OR IN ANY PART,
BY MIMEOGRAPH OR ANY OTHER MEANS,
WITHOUT WRITTEN PERMISSION FROM THE PUBLISHER.

SUN PUBLISHING
1447 PEACHTREE STREET • ATLANTA, GEORGIA 30309

CONTENTS

FOREWORD 1
WELCOME TO THE CARNIVAL ... 6
THE BUSINESS 12
(QUESTIONS AND ANSWERS)
CARNY TALK 30
THE GAMES 41
    HANKY PANK 43
    SKILL GAMES 53
    GROUP GAMES 61
    PERCENTAGE 67
    BUILD UP 75
    ALIBI GAMES 79
    FLAT STORE 95
BEHIND THE SCENES 105
MONEY • MONEY • MONEY 115
THE FIXER 129
THE NEWS 139

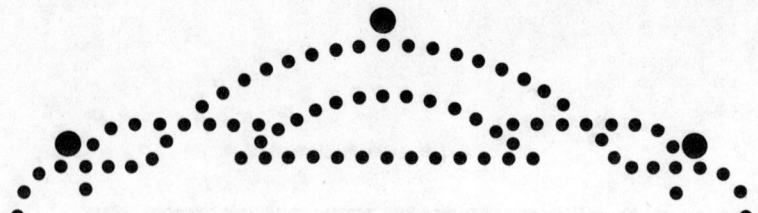

"I have researched every book on this subject in the library and your knowledge exceeds them all — therefore I urge you to write a book on carnivals."
Sgt. Bob Cantwell
Colorado Organized Crime Strike Force

"Gene certainly knows how the games are rigged."
Ed Greenan, Investigators Dir.
Illinois State Police

"We appreciate the awareness brought to us by you in a field that little was known."
John Wynn, Agnet
Georgia Bureau of Investigation

"I commend him for his deeds but I don't like Gene's percentages for living."
Det. Carl Shoffler
Washington, D.C. Police Dept.

"He's got a level of expertise in this area that we simply don't have."
Michael Mihm, State Attorney
Peoria County, Illinois

"After years of practicing the trade of frauding the public, you are to be commended for your efforts in helping law enforcement to end this problem."
Tom Heffernan, Investigator
District Attorney's Office — Sacramento, California

"This department is indebted to you for your efforts to make us aware of a problem that has long been overlooked."
Captain Bradley Pope
Georgia's Cobb County Police

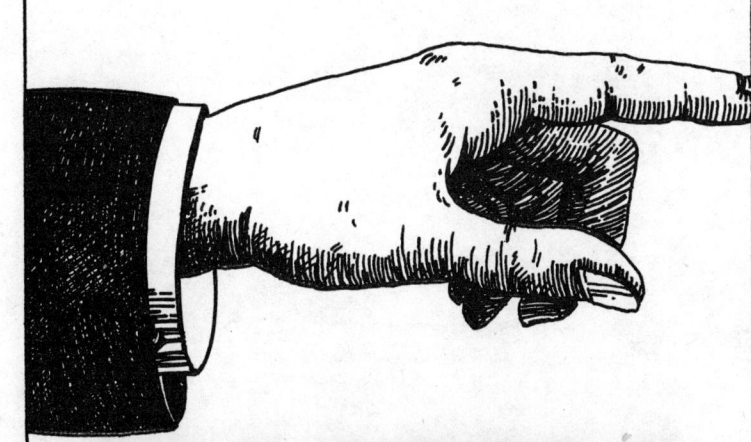

FOREWORD

SAVE THE CARNIVAL

For most of the fifteen years associated with the carnival industry, my life as a Carny was one of indescribable satisfaction and... No, the truth is that it was just plain fun. But then, isn't that what carnivals are supposed to be? Maybe that is why I feel no remorse in terming that life in the past tense, for as sure as I'm gone (for the most part), so has the fun. Yes, the Carny world I grew to love as a wide-eyed and very naive fifteen-year-old is no more. The "one for all, and all for one" existence of a colorful band of nomads has gradually transformed into a cold and calculated struggle that unless checked, threatens to drive into extinction one of the few remaining "frontiers". The Carny world is in trouble, the Carnies know it, and yet they stand idly by. That is, all but one.

"EX-CARNIE, WRITING BOOK, SPELLS TROUBLE", is the way the carnival trade magazine described my new role. Personally, I describe it, R-E-L-I-E-F. Then, as now, I feel the relief of speaking out against the atrocities that victimize not only the carnival patron, but the Carny as well. Those atrocities, my friend, are un-American.

Carnivals are America. They're as much a part of our heritage as "apple pie and chevrolet". They're cotton candy and big stuffed animals. They're the rides and the games. Like Easter, Independence Day, Thanksgiving and Christmas, they're a holiday. They're Fair Week, something new and exciting coming to town each year. Now isn't that worth preserving?

Let's save – for our children, their children, and their children's children – the joy and excitement that only the Carnival can offer. Let's save that "wild mustang" nomad that is the *real* Carny and whose sole purpose is centered around one thing – entertainment. And how?

Ben Franklin said it best. "Problems are like thieves. When well investigated, they often disappear." A close investigation of the enormously secretive world of spinning rides is long over-due and, since even legitimate Carnies are burdened with an allegiance to a ridiculous "Code of Silence", it is up to you.

But to solve a problem, one must first understand it. This is the reason for my book, and this is my role; my only role. I am not the "Moses of the Carnival", nor do I wish to be. I am not an Ex-Carny, nor do I wish to be. I am merely a man who fell in love with the greatest form of outdoor entertainment in history and will do everything within my capabilities, and use everything at my disposal, including breaking the "Code of Silence" to divulge every unknown fact, in order to "SAVE THE CARNIVAL!"

WELCOME TO THE CARNIVAL

7

> "She sprang to life in '94
> This Lady strong and proud
> With food, and games, and rides galore
> And laughter ringing loud"

Step right up folks, and enjoy the company of a grand old friend – the carnival!

She has many faces, this "grand lady of entertainment." At one time the carnival consists of a few games and rides nestled in the corner of a shopping center; and the next time, it is the mile-long midway of a State Fair. But one part of her never changes, and that is an unequalled ability to captivate the joys and imaginations of children from six to sixty. Like the Pied Piper, she gathers millions to her breast each year with the simple call of, "the carnival is coming!" She is "show business" in the truest sense.

The midway is her stage and each sibling has his part: from the prop men erecting the huge riding devices to the actors delivering their lines behind the counters of the game booths. They are all a part of the play; a play that for decades has drawn rave reviews from each stop along the circuit.

And yet the questions coming from carnival patrons are quite humorous. It simply amazes me that so many people, many of whom I know are far more educated than myself, are unaware about something so ever-present as the carnival industry. Granted, the knowledge of how the games work, especially the rigged games, is kept from them because Carnies are supposed to hold them ignorant. But it is the little things that I find humorous; questions like, "What does that teddy bear really cost?" or "Are you a Gypsy?"

Well, let me start off by saying that, regardless of what the smooth-talker behind the game counter says, that teddy bear costs him about two bucks, and that big dog called a SPOOFER costs, at the most, fifteen dollars. And, no, all Carnies are *not* Gypsies, although quite a few Gypsies can be found among the carnival ranks. But the question that really amazes me is the feeling that all Carnies are homeless vagabonds sleeping in trucks. As for this image, it might interest you to know that there are more middle-class or even upper-class Carnies than the so-called "Gypsy." I personally always stayed at the best motels and, if the mood struck, could always afford a hundred dollars or so on any given night for a little "wining and dining."

One carny with such a deceiving image comes to mind. To look at Mark-the-Barf (his Carny name) you would swear the guy hadn't eaten in a week and that his clothes had come from the local mission store. The latter part is true, for indeed, his wardrobe always came from the local thrift stores. But a homeless vagabond? Carnies are as unique in character as they are in their nicknames and, believe me, Mark-the-Barf was a unique character. One of the best rigged-game operators in the business, he made plenty of money, but he wouldn't spend it; or should I say, he held onto it at least until the carnival season was over and it was time to head to Florida for the winter months. Then he would count out his freshly-ironed season's savings (yes, believe it or not, he actually ironed his money, which would be ten to fifteen thousand dollars after the season's expenses), go to Florida, buy a boat, and do nothing all winter but lie back and fish. When it was time for the start of the next carnival season, he'd sell the boat and hit the road. Not too shabby a life for a "homeless vagabond," huh? (And you might ask how he got the dubious handle of the "Barf": it was because he simply had no scruples about cleanliness. I mean, the guy actually named the cockroaches in his Cadillac!)

Yes, there are many fascinating characters such as Mark. Their names are Buttermilk, Baldy, Mayonnaise, Bad-eye Freddie, Dirtyneck Harry, George-the-Worm, Bloodtest Dave, No-Shoes Red, Pill-Head Ronnie, Crazy Dave and Dennis-the-Menace and they live in the carnival world, filled with as many interesting facts as there are spinning rides. (More about them in another book!)

THE BUSINESS

HOW MANY CARNIVALS ARE THERE?

When speaking of the number of different carnival companies, believe it or not, even the Carnies don't know! Depending on the source, the number ranges from five to seven hundred, or more. But then again, on many occasions, it is quite difficult to determine just what constitutes a legitimate carnival company.

ARE THERE DIFFERENT TYPES OF CARNIVALS?

Normally, carnival companies are broken into three categories: small, intermediate and major. However, on one occasion a certain "carnival company" was a far cry from the "normal." I played this particular engagement on a dusty lot in South Carolina and the only type of riding device was a Ferris Wheel that wouldn't turn. It was merely used to attract what turned out to be a fairly good crowd for the dozen or so rigged games scattered about. Could this be considered a "carnival company"? But seriously, carnival companies are, for the most part, broken into three categories.

As much as I hate to single out any of the three as more likely to carry rigged games, there is no getting around the fact that more of these deceptive devices are found within the category of small carnivals. Why? Competition is the name of the game and even a carnival carrying a couple dozen assorted major rides (Merry-Go-Round, Ferris Wheel, Tilt-O-Whirl, etc.) along with kiddie rides, finds itself playing the smaller county fairs which draw smaller crowds and therefore, mean smaller profits. Many small carnival company owners feel they need an edge to overcome the sometimes sparse crowds and, I don't care what anybody says, a good thief behind the counter of a rigged game can generate revenues in a hurry. Usually with this type of operation, the owner of the carnival also owns the rigged games or at least is "cut in on the action." Therefore, as one carnival owner bluntly stated, and I quote, "There is no way I can stay in business without running Flat Stores," unquote. Other owners of small carnivals just don't care about the appearance or the condition of their operations. These operations are called "Rag bags" and, believe me, the name fits. But let me stress that by no means should a small carnival be categorized as being dishonest or unkept just because of its size. There are numerous companies that take pride in their operation and go to great lengths to offer the public what carnivals are supposed to offer – good, clean, family entertainment.

The intermediate carnival companies carry not only a large selection of major and kiddie rides but one of the huge riding devices referred to as a "Spectacular". These would be such rides as the: Double Ferris Wheel, Sky Wheel, Hymalaya, etc. Because of these "Spectaculars", the intermediate carnival is able to obtain the larger county fair contracts and occasionally, a state fair contract.

The major carnivals are the "mile-long" spreads found at the majority of state fairs. These operations are truly big business with ride investments alone that run into the millions of dollars. Like any other large company, a major carnival may carry hundreds of employees with an annual payroll of well over a half-million dollars. Maybe that is why more and more of these huge conglomerates have joined the computer age and actually carry a computer and an operator during their seasonal trek.

In the early days, any carnival that carried the three big rides – the Merry-Go-Round, the Ferris Wheel, and the Whip – was considered "major". Today, a carnival many times carries a single ride costing a quarter-million dollars or more. So whether it is small, intermediate or major, today's carnival industry is indeed, big business.

HOW IS A CARNIVAL SET UP?

The overall layout is called the Midway, or Lot and is broken into two sections: the front and back end. The front end is the area where the majority of concession booths can be found. The reason for this is that the visitors will have to go by these booths first in order to get to the rides and side shows (which the Carny knows will always get their fair share of business).

ARE THERE DIFFERENT PRICES FOR EACH BOOTH?

There are three types of concessions: the games, the food booths, and the straight sales. The game booths usually lined down both sides of the midway, as well as in the middle, are called JOINTS. The games along the sides are called LINE-UPS and the middle concession's are called CENTERS. For some reason, carnival patrons have a tendency to walk to the right when entering a midway and concession owners try hard for a location on the right-hand side, and thus for the first opportunity at potential players. The left-hand side of the midway is called a "doniker" location because the chances of catching fresh players are diminished greatly. (You see, a DONIKER is the term used by Carnies for a bathroom or outhouse.) Unlike the other two concessions, game concessions are usually charged a certain amount per frontal foot by the carnival owner as rent. (Example: If the rent is $20 per frontal foot and the length along the front of the particular booth measures ten feet, the concession owner owes $200 in rent. For a concession owner with a number of games booked at a state fair, his rent can become quite expensive. Some space goes for as much as $100 per frontal foot and in such engagements, if a concession owner puts up ten concessions, totaling 100 frontal feet, his rent would be $10,000 whether it rains or shines.) The CENTER JOINTS are usually charged for a side-and-a-half, i.e., ten feet plus five, for a total of fifteen frontal feet.

There are numerous varieties of food concessions, but the three most popular are the: COOKHOUSES, GRAB JOINTS and the POPPERS. The POPPERS are the popcorn and cotton candy booths. The COOKHOUSE is the huge, cafeteria-style concession where the patron can sit and enjoy his food. The majority of Cookhouses are there for the convenience of the Carnies. The GRAB JOINTS are the smaller booths scattered around the Midway offering such items as hot dogs, hamburgers, sausages and corn dogs. Usually these booths offer no seats and thus you have to *grab* a hot dog and move on. Of the three, the Popper is the most profitable for its owner, but also the hardest to book. A food concession, more times than not, is charged a percentage of what it takes in; and before you ask, the answer is yes, the food owner can cheat the carnival owner as to how much he takes in. But there are no contracts when concessions are booked and the concession owner knows that if he gets too greedy, there is no shortage of other concessions ready and willing to up the count. As for "how clean is the food found on a Midway?" I have mixed feelings, but there is a definite need for more stringent health guidelines.

STRAIGHT SALES pretty well speak for themselves. The most popular, as well as the most profitable, I would have to say, are the iron-on T-shirt concessions. Though it sometimes varies, these types of concessions most always are charged a set amount for rent.

●● 17 ●●●

WHO ARE THOSE MEN WHO TALK LOUD TO GET MY ATTENTION?

One interesting concession sometimes found tucked discreetly somewhere to the side of the front end is the JAM AUCTION. It takes on the appearance of a medicine show where the BARKER does various magic tricks to draw in a crowd. Once this is done, the show begins. First the JAMMER, as he is called, will pass out free products such as rain bonnets, ink pens, etc. The reason for this generosity is two-fold: first, it relaxes the crowd, instilling the thought of getting something for nothing; and second, it gives an opening for the sales pitch.

As the eager hands grasp the trinkets, the Jammer begins, "Ladies and Gentlemen, you might ask yourself how I can afford to give these gifts away? Well, the answer is simple. You see, I work for a major distributor who has decided to bypass the outrageous costs of commercial advertising and offer you, the customer, unbelievable savings. Now how many of you bargain hunters have a dollar bill? The "lucky" people who pass up their dollar bills receive boxes containing pen and pencil sets which the Jammer says are worth $10.95!

Such "bargains" continue until the final items, several large heavy cartons, are wheeled onto the stage. "Who in the audience will give me $80 for what's in this box?" The crowd grows silent, for even though the merchandise so far has been well worth the investment, and the huge box before them is tempting, $80 is $80!

This is the finale – the moment of truth – and the time when the Jammer earns his pay.

"Who will trust me for this unbelievable bargain? Who will be the lucky few to walk away with the buy of a lifetime?" Slowly the hands pop up and the money is collected. With perfect timing, the Jammer rips away the carton, revealing a do-everything sewing machine with a lifetime guarantee. "The retail value? Over $400!"

Sure it is. And the price of gas is still thirty cents a gallon!

The do-everything sewing machine *might* have cost him twenty dollars. The pen and pencil set *might* have cost a quarter. The chances of success with the "lifetime guarantee" are about the same as that of winning one of the rigged games! If ever confronted with a faulty purchase, the smiling Jammer will be more than sympathetic, but he will claim that he is just the promotions man, helpless to right the problem.

My advice is to stay for the free act, but when the rain bonnets are pulled out, seek another part of the Midway!

WHERE ARE THE SHOWS LOCATED?

The back end of the Midway houses the bulk of the entertainment. In all my carnival years, which were spent totally at the front end with the games, the back end was always my favorite. It still is, especially at night. The lights... the sounds... the only word I can use to describe it is... *magic*. Literally thousands of multi-colored bulbs illuminate the rides while the thrillseekers are screaming and laughing. Rock'n'Roll music blares from the Spectaculars and synchronizes perfectly with the Barkers making their spiels from the side shows. Even the dancers, offering a hint of what can be expected inside the girly revue, seem innocent. This, to me, is the true excitement of the carnival. But even here there can be problems. A perfect example is the difference between two entirely different girly shows – a revue and a skin show – with the difference being in the amount of visable flesh.

The real revues are, for the most part, a thing of the past, and, in my opinion, it is a shame. Certainly these extravaganzas were geared to burlesque, with the dancers offering a glimpse of pasties and g-strings, but they were also quite entertaining, whether it be to a young soldier or to a grandmother.

A SKIN SHOW is exactly that. Found mostly on carnivals that carry an abundance of rigged games, these shows have essentially two purposes: to draw potential male victims to the rigged games; and, after they have been taken, if necessary, to "soothe" the hurt from the fleecing.

More than once, while working a FLAT STORE, (given its name because you can flat out rob somebody), I stopped a potential player hurrying to a skin show by waving a "free game" ticket and calling, "You've got to have one of these to get into the show!"

Whenever an enticement such as a Skin Show is nestled in the back end of a Midway, you can be assured that, more times than not, a Flat Store will be close by. This is for three reasons: first, if the MARKS (the Carny's name for carnival patrons) are waiting for the next show to begin, there is a chance of getting them to play; second, when leaving the show, they will usually be in a good mood and therefore, more vulnerable, and third, if a Flat Store operator really takes a player and thinks the player might complain, he can scribble his initials on one of the free game tickets, send him back to the show, and the girls know to give the disgruntled loser whatever special "treatment" it might take to cool him off. If the "treatment" is successful (which it almost always is), the Skin Show owner visits the game operator later to return the ticket and pick up ten percent of whatever amount the Mark was clipped for. Half he keeps, while the rest goes to the girl who offered the treatment. But to the game operator, giving up the ten percent is a wise investment, for many a complaint has been settled with a Skin Show. Sometimes the girl who gets the 5% lives with the game operator so he, in essence, only gives up 5% instead of 10%.

So even in the back end, where even I found myself captivated, there lurk problems.

HOW MANY CARNIVAL ENGAGEMENTS ARE PLAYED EACH YEAR?

Once again, no one knows! A comprehensive guide, which is relied upon by numerous Carnies, lists over 2500 engagements. Although this is impressive, it is also quite deceiving. No listing can be found of the thousands of low-priority engagements such as the ones held at shopping centers, church bazaars, celebrations, military posts, and small towns like Conyers, Georgia.

HOW MANY PEOPLE PATRONIZE CARNIVALS EACH YEAR?

I know it sounds like a recording but, once again, no one knows. Relying on more than one source, the attendance of just the top 100 fairs in the United States and Canada exceeds 54 million people, and remember, that is just the top 100 of probably well over 2500!

DID YOU KNOW THAT A SIMPLE FORTUNE TELLING BOOTH CAN MANY TIMES BE MORE COSTLY TO AN UNSUSPECTING PATRON THAN ANY RIGGED GAME?

Called a MITT CAMP, this scam operation operates like this: The female "Gypsy Reader" sizes up a potential victim very carefully, favoring a man wearing a wedding band. When she has found just the right target, she nestles close to the table, giving him the opportunity to see that she is wearing nothing under her loose-fitting blouse. When she knows that his attention is on her breasts (and not on whether he will live to be a hundred), she begins. With the appearance of being in a trance, her body begins to weave and the top of her dress reveals even more. "Your problems are financial," she moans, "I can feel it. Your money is cursed, I must bless it." With this she may simply ask for his wallet. But if her customer needs a little more working-on, she will take his hand and place it on her nearly exposed breast or thigh. This is usually all it takes for the victim to hurriedly remove his billfold from a back pocket with one hand (while carefully leaving the other in place). With a skill developed from countless hours of practice, the Reader places a handkerchief over the wallet and, in the blink of an eye, she removes whatever bills she can. After the transfer is made, the wallet is returned. A few more "feels" are allowed, and the victim is guided out much lighter than the five bucks which the Reader was careful to collect in advance. Chances are he will never think of his "blessed money" but rather of the thrills he experienced during the "hypnotic" state of the Reader. There was the time, however, that an Alabama fellow discovered that he was $40 short after a "reading" and called the cops. This is where the male Gypsy, presumably the father of the fortune-teller, does his part. "I want him arrested," the father screamed. "My daughter say he play with her breast. She only fourteen!" The thought of going to jail for molesting a child quickly made the married Mark remember he had spent the $40 somewhere else. Of course, a Gypsy wife works just as well, for molesting any female can become quite a dilemma.

DID YOU KNOW THAT TWO CARNIES CAN BE LEGALLY MARRIED (AT LEAST IN THE EYES OF THEIR PEERS) WITH THE HELP OF A CARNIVAL RIDE?

It's true! When a couple wishes to tie the knot, they don't call on a Preacher but on a Ferris Wheel operator. One turn around the wheel is all it takes to make the couple happy ever after. But divorces are sometimes desired and all that's needed to untie the knot is a turn backwards on the same wheel.

DID YOU KNOW THAT CARNIES ARE AMONG THE MOST SUPERSTITIOUS PEOPLE IN THE WORLD?

If you want to stir the ire of a Carny just stand under a game awning while eating peanuts. And a game operator who wears a yellow shirt is considered such bad luck that he will be asked to "take the day off." Playing to anyone who is crippled or afflicted is also taboo to Carnies. Even taking money from someone with a broken leg is thought to produce bad luck. Speaking of bad luck, would you want a converted ambulance to park in your back yard? Well, Carnies, who often convert old ambulances or hearses into campers, do not allow those on the fairgrounds either.

●● 23 ●●

DID YOU KNOW THAT THE SMILING "HELPER" BEHIND THE COUNTER OF A RIGGED GAME RECEIVES, AS HIS PAY, HALF OF EVERY DOLLAR HE TAKES IN?

That's right! That "helper" is called an AGENT and if you've ever dropped a hundred bucks trying to win that big stuffed dog, you've contributed $50 to the Agent's hotel bill and perhaps a few scotch-and-water's. But don't think for a minute that he doesn't appreciate it!

HOW MUCH CAN AN AGENT MAKE IN A SEASON?

There is no set amount and believe it or not, for the life of me, I can't remember my best year! What I do remember is taking $2750 off one player and making over $4000 in one engagement. But as unique as the Carny names, so are the variables that determine the difference in a profitable and not so profitable season. In other words, an Agent can make, say, $40,000 during the season and yet wind up with nothing for the winter. How? Habits!

I worked a rigged game one year at the Southeastern Fair in Atlanta and not only watched my fellow Agent shoot heroin while playing a Mark, but saw him fly out three times during the ten-day event to purchase more. This guy made a ton of money, but it all went into his veins.

And then there was Rocking Rollo. He also was a good Agent and made plenty of money, but he had a variety of "habits" which included drugs, booze and women. The latter left him with a permanent reminder when, after propositioning a prostitute by flashing a huge roll of $100 bills, her pimp shot him in the rump. He survived, and so did his habits.

For other Agents the ultimate vice is gambling and I've seen dice and card games with pots containing ten's of thousands of dollars.

But one thing is certain, even a mediocre Agent can make a better-than-average living only working six to eight months a year and he usually doesn't report a dime to the IRS. That's right!

WHAT ENGAGEMENTS ARE THE MOST PROFITABLE FOR AN AGENT?

Some Agents prefer playing a state fair, even though the grueling routine, of fifteen-hour days for ten days straight, takes its toll. The reason is quite simple. With the huge crowds, an Agent is assured of grossing from $300 to $500 a day, which also assures him of leaving the engagement with anywhere from $1500 to $2500.

Other Agents prefer the "sure money" found at military bases on payday, or found in poor areas at the first of the month. Whether it is a soldier's pay, a welfare check or (as distasteful as it sounds) food stamps, the hours are much shorter, and the Marks are not only plentiful but, for some reason, seem to be more gullible.

Agents— they're truly a special breed. Though in reality they are little more than sophisticated thieves steadily searching for the next hustle, they could also be listed among the elite, super salesmen of the world. Just think about this for a minute. If a Carny Agent can talk a grown man out of $200 for a $2 teddy bear, can you imagine what he could do with a legitimate deal? Before a used car salesman, a vacuum cleaner salesman, or real estate wheeler-dealer, I'd put my money on a Carny Agent any time. They are so resourceful!

25

Agents can always find a way to turn a buck, and don't think it has to be on a carnival Midway. For years Agents worked their rigged games from the innocent confines of pecan stands in Southeast Georgia. And in South Carolina it was the nudie bars. Yes, they are indeed resourceful. So if you ever pull into a truck stop and a smiling gentleman offers you a "free chance" at a new set of radials, don't even risk a look at the strange looking game device on the trunk of his car!

You might have noticed that I have referred to Agents thus far in the masculine gender. In all my carnival years, I never heard of more than a few female Agents. However, one time I worked a game with a female, and I saw clearly that she had an "edge" over her male counterparts. There was no way that I, or the other two male Agents, could keep up with her. She had each male customer eagerly reaching for his wallet with one hand, without removing the other hand she had allowed to be placed on one of her breasts. In every case, they would pay whatever she charged for the next chance at the game. She was something else, that gal, but we decided she could be something else, somewhere else. I never saw her again, but I'm sure she made out all right.

DID YOU KNOW THAT THREE MEN WITH NO PREVIOUS CARNIVAL TIES EMERGED TO BECOME PROMINENT FIGURES IN THE ANNALS OF CARNVAL HISTORY?

"Buffalo Bill" Cody will be forever remembered as a frontier hero, but he was also the first president of the oldest carnival organization, the *Showman's League of America*. George Ferris is remembered as a famous bridge builder, but anyone visiting a Midway will see that he devised the first modern carnival ride, the popular Ferris Wheel. But a quiet man of Germanic ancestry is probably the most important and least remembered of them all. For it was Otto Schmidt, a former scenic artist at a Chicago theatre, who formed the first traveling carnival in 1894.

When the World's Columbian Exposition made its debut in Chicago on May 1, 1893, it is quite possible that the man destined to become the "Father of the Traveling Carnival" headed the line of the half-million first-day visitors. He was extremely infatuated with the huge events and those strange characters known as "outdoor showmen."

Well before that time (even before the Civil War) various "entertainment merchants" had appeared at the various fairs scattered throughout the country. Historians may argue that it was the famous P.T. Barnum, and not Otto Schmidt, who founded the first traveling carnival. In all honesty, some of Barnum's circuses in the 1850's may have given the appearance of carnivals, but these circuses proved unsatisfactory for the outdoor showmen. The experiment was short-lived and after its demise, the early-day Carnies once more became unorganized independents.

The Columbian Exposition, was the largest assembly, to date, of those early Carnies and it provided the first opportunity for them to find solutions to their common problems.

The Midway Plaisance, an area where many of the showmen pitched their tents, was also the first coordinated "booking" of space. To many showmen, the accepted procedure before this fair had been just to "show up" and grab whatever space could be found. Which was less than desirable and, for the most part, outright chaotic. So, with the introduction of this coordinated booking system, the fair turned out to be very pleasant, as well as profitable, even though it was during the 1890 depression.

But there were problems. After the Exposition opened, *The Chicago Tribune* began a summer-long, front-page attack on Carnies that left its readers with the impression that all Carnies were ripoff artists. This was a problem for the legitimate showman trying to make a living, not only at the Exposition but at any other fair he might work.

For these reasons, showmen began meeting in large numbers to discuss the idea of forming planned midways or traveling carnivals. As a group, they could not only eliminate the random appearance of the "lucky boys", thus avoiding the stigma of the conniving Carny, but they could regulate the quality and quantity of attractions offered at each engagement which, of course, would add to the profits for all. The idea won the favor of an overwhelming number of independent showmen, but there was one slight hitch: no showman seemed willing to take the initiative.

It is ironic that a non-showman would emerge from the shadows and grasp the reins of leadership, but Otto Schmidt did just that. And so, during 1894, there was born the "traveling carnival."

In fact, Schmidt was one of two non-showmen who would emerge from the 1893-84 World's Columbian Exposition into a prominent role in the history of the carnival industry. The other was the bridge-builder George Ferris who, through his creation of the famous wheel ride, saved the carnival from financial disaster.

If these two men had pooled their innovations, the first traveling carnivals would no doubt have been financially successful. But like the "pre-wheel" days of the Exposition, the initial outings offered by Schmidt had no single attraction to draw crowds – the first carnivals had no Ferris Wheels or other rides. It was not until the introduction of riding devices, such as the Ferris Wheel, that this young industry showed any real signs of growth and prosperity. By 1903, there were over twenty traveling carnivals crisscrossing the country. At this time another pioneer made his mark. A ride builder by the name of C.W. Parker brought out a carnival so large that it required twenty-six railroad cars for transport. But it was his innovative method of utilizing a steam engine to furnish his carnival with lighting that was so important. Considering that the crude midway introduced by Schmidt had consisted of sparse lighting from skillet-like oil pans, this was indeed a milestone in the life of this young "lady."

Otto Schmidt, like most pioneers, would not benefit from his initiative. But without his leadership, carnivals may not have developed into the organized industry they are today.

CARNY TALK

"Pick a lucky duck" – "Two in, wins!" – "High and dry" – "Did you get your free game ticket?"

Anyone visiting a carnival has heard such calls ringing from the game booths, but which ones should be answered? It all depends on your chances of winning and, for many games, you have no chance for a decent prize! But which ones are the best to play? I'll let you in on a few tips.

Before I get into describing the games, you need to know some of the "Carny talk" used around the games. To prohibit outsiders from understanding what they are saying, Carnies use either the following vocabulary or a fast volley of "Pig Latin." (A conversation between Carnies is termed "cutting up jackpots.") Even with all my years in the business, I frequently found myself lost in such a conversation.

Here is some of the basic terminology:

ACE – A dollar.

AFRICAN DIP – A game that, although it issues no prize, is one of the most popular. The customer throws baseballs at a target protruding from a cage with someone perched inside. The caged person heckles the player, and a good hit gives the player the satisfaction of seeing the insult-tosser dropped into a tank of water. The name African Dip comes from early years when a black man was perched inside. During that era the majority of carnival visitors were whites and the opportunity of putting an "uppity black in his place" was quite appealing. Today's version is referred to as a BOZO, with the prejudice being replaced by the acceptable appearance of a clown, but the barrage of insults directed at the player is still the key to its popularity.

ALIBI – The excuse any Agent uses to void a legitimate win. The most common Alibi is to tell the player he went over the foul line, but you can believe that the Agent will find some excuse to keep from paying off.

ALIBI AGENT – The quick thinking Agent who is always ready to show a player what he did wrong.

ALIBI GAMES – Rigged games where sometimes, through a malfunction by either the Agent or the device that controls the outcome, an alibi has to be used to avoid issuing a choice prize. The most common Alibi Game is the BUSHEL BASKETS where the idea is to toss softballs into a peach basket. If the balls stay in, a choice prize is supposed to be awarded. Even though the chances of this occurring are next to impossible, on a rare occasion a player will beat the odds. But to his dismay he finds that he has violated one of the two built-in Alibies of "crossing the foul line" or "hitting the red rim" on the outer edge of the basket first.

ALIBI KOOK – An Agent that works nothing but Alibi Games. One reason for this preference is that some Agents just like this particular type of game. Another reason is that they may not have what it takes to work the more sophisticated games and, since Alibi Games are allowed to play to teenagers, some Agents feel more at ease robbing a player under eighteen.

BAT AWAY – When rigged games are in operation and there is no chance of Agents being arrested, the orders are given to take a player's money anyway possible or to Bat Away. I have worked under such orders and have seen Agents literally reach into a player's wallet and take his money, knowing that the poor guy had little chance of getting satisfaction from the uniformed cop standing by.

BEEF – A complaint from a customer which usually rises from the rigged games.

BLANK – A player who isn't worth bothering with. Example: "What a Blank that bum was. He looked like he had money, but all he had was three lousy bucks!"

BLOW – To malfunction, as in the device that rigs a game; also, to give out a prize in order to entice a crowd.

BONUS – An important ploy. To entice a player to continue playing a rigged game, a Bonus is given. Example: "Good for you, sir, you just hit a Bonus! Now you really have something to play for, because now you not only get a chance at a big stuffed animal, but a hundred bucks of the boss' money!" A player winds up with a Bonus by the Agent mis-calling a number or when a ring goes half way over the block that has to be entirely encircled in order to win. Many a player would walk away after a couple of games without the added incentive of somehow hitting a Bonus.

BOOST – To steal.

BR – The money, or BIG ROLL, an Agent uses to rob a player. As important a tool as the device which rigs the game, the scam is to make a player think that the big roll of bills being flashed by the Agent will soon be his because of something he did during the game. Example: "Congratulations, sir, now when you win, you not only get...." All the time nothing but green is shoved in the player's face. This not only starts the player's adrenalin flowing, but also serves as a diversion away from how the game might be rigged.

CANVAS JOINT – A game that is housed in a portable canvas-and-frame shack. It is set up and torn down at each engagement. These hinged frames can vary in price from $1000 for a fourteen-footer, to over $4000 for a huge center stand.

CENTER JOINT – The games located down the middle of the Midway that usually cater to more than one player at a time. Most carnivals charge the owners of these games 50% more for space than the ones lined along the side.

CHART – A graph that is on a 8"x12" card. It is placed on the counter of Count Stores and shows what scores are worth how many points. The player looks at the card while he plays, allowing the Agent the chance to miscount the totals. The graph is used to victimize a player. The numbers which are scored most often do not have any value in points on the graph. (See Count Store games.)

CLERK – Although some Agents are referred to as Clerks, this term usually applies to the less-skilled game operator whose main responsibility is to make change. A Clerk is often found in legitimate games and receives 25% of what he brings in as pay.

COP – The word used by a Carny when a rigged game malfunctions. "This game is Copped!"

COUNT STORE – A rigged game in which the Agent uses a fast-count technique to keep the player in the game. As the player gets more points he wants to put down more money to win bigger and bigger prizes. (Which he will never collect, of course!)

CRADLE – The hidden device, such as a pedal, by which some rigged games are manipulated.

DEALER – A carnival operator who works a percentage game such as a dice table. Women are frequently used as Dealers and receive a third of what they bring in, with another third going to the game owner and the rest to the carnival owner.

DOUBLE – Twenty dollars.

DUCKET – Something used to help get a player into a game such as a free game card or a token souvenir. Regardless of its form, a Ducket is merely a com-on. A Ducket can be an important ploy to an Agent when he really takes a player. The disgruntled player is sent with a free pass to the Girlie Show, and when the ticket taker sees the Ducket he knows what has happened and what must be done to cool him off. What is a better cooler than to make sure the cooperative girls give him a little extra attention? After the "mooch" is satisfied and has left, the Ducket is taken back to the Agent along with a bill for "services rendered."

DUKE SHOT – The way an Agent allows a customer to win, either by slight of hand or by the device that controls the game.

EMBY – A term used for a gullible player.

END – The amount of the gross a game operator gets for his pay.

FAIRBANK – The ploy used by an Agent to give the player a token sum of money to keep him in the game.

FEATURE – The rigged game an Agent works best.

FIN – Five dollars.

FLASH – The merchandise on display in a game booth.

FLASH CLOTH – Colorful cloth drapes and counter covers used inside a booth for cosmetic purposes often hiding the rigging and devices that control who wins.

FLAT STORE – The most deadly group of rigged games; so-called because, with these games, an Agent can "flat out" rob a player.

FLATTIE – The Agent that works a Flat Store. These are the elite rigged game operators who prey on players of obvious upper income levels. A Flattie is one of the most sophisticated salesmen in the world. I once saw a Flattie take a dentist for over $4000! A Flattie is well respected by his fellow Carnies and is offered special treatment such as working fewer hours than the rest of the game operators, having someone to set up and tear down his booth, and having a person ready to run errands for him.

GAFF – Any variety of devices used by the Carny to rig his game so that a player cannot win. A Gaff can be a spring, an added shelf, or a basket.

GIGGING – The process used by an Agent to get all of a player's money on one try. The step-by-step process of beating a player gradually is considered a work of art, and a good Agent such as a Flattie prides himself with this skill. Therefore the practice of Gigging is frowned upon by these professionals. Also see GIG SHOT.

GIG ARTIST – An Agent who lacks the finesse of beating a player without causing a complaint or an Agent that simply enjoys Gigging. If an Agent is ever labeled a Gig Artist, it is hard for him to find work, except in the most frowned-upon carnival operations.

GIG SHOT – The manipulation by which an Agent gigs a player. The Agent does this when he suddenly goes from asking 25¢ per try to asking $20, $50 or $100 per try.

GRIND STORE – Another name for a Flat Store.

HALF YARD – Fifty dollars.

HANDLE – See Gaff.

HANKY PANK – A game that can be won, but the prize issued is usually small, such as a plastic ring, etc. Even though a player usually wins every time, there is still some Hanky Panky as to the size of the prize.

HYPE – When an Agent asks a player for more money.

IN THE SADDLE – When a player reaches 99 yards while playing a Flat Store.

KB – When an Agent has to give a complaining customer his money back, he refers to the money given back as a KB (Kick Back).

KICK – The money a Carny keeps in his pocket.

LAY BEAR – A stuffed animal given to a woman, frequently a teenager, who trades sexual favors for a furry teddy bear. Such an exchange is quite acceptable to the Carny because the bear costs him three dollars at the most.

LAYDOWN – The counter where a player places his wager.

LAYING IT DOWN – Explaining the game to a player.

LIVE ONE – A player with a lot of money or easy to beat.

LOSUM GAME – A lousy game. Example: If an Agent thinks a player might complain or the player has already been beaten, he will tip off his co-worker by telling him Losum Game. The worker knows immediately to end the game.

MARK – A game customer or other outsider. See MOOCH.

MB – Sometimes an Agent will offer a player his Money Back, along with a prize, when he wins to aid his chances of robbing him. This ploy is called MB'ing a player.

MONEY STORE – A game that works strictly for money.

MOOCH – A customer. Particularly a player whose anger at losing has been dissipated by a Ducket trip to the Girlie Show.

OUTSIDE MAN – Some games require a Carny on the *outside* of the booth to work the device that rigs the game.

PEEK STORE – A variation of a Flat Store. (See GAME section.)

PERCENTAGE JOINT – Also called a PC JOINT, these games depend on a certain volume of players for their profits.

PLUSH – Stuffed animals such as teddy bears.

PUNK – A child.

PUNK ROBBER – An Agent that plays to children.

RACKET – The general term for all the con devices that Carnies use as games or deceptions to get money. (See GAMES section.)

RACKET SHOW – A carnival that carries rigged games.

RAG – A small stuffed prize in a plastic bag. Being the usual prize given in games large quantities are kept under the counter.

REHASH – To replay a customer on the same game or recirculate used ride tickets.

SAWBUCK – Ten dollars.

SCORE – When an Agent takes a player for more than a hundred dollars.

SEND MARK – When a Mark runs out of money while playing a game, an Agent will Send him home for more. Example: "Put your initials on this score sheet, sir, and I'll hold the game while you step off for enough money to finish your game."

SKILL GAME – A game where the player, through his own ability, can win a decent prize.

SLUM – Cheap prizes such as combs, whistles, plastic rings, etc. The price of SLUM can vary from a little over a dollar to almost ten dollars per gross wholesale.

SPOOFER – The big stuffed dog in a game. The price of Spoofers range from $10 to $15 each wholesale.

STICK – A Carny that pretends to be an Outsider and a winner.

STING – When an Agent beats a player for less than a hundred dollars.

STOCK – Prizes displayed all over the booth apparently to be won in a game.

STORE – A booth operating a rigged game.

SUCKER – An outsider.

THROW OUT – The prize which an Agent sometimes "arranges" for a player to win to help bring in more customers.

TIP – A ready or repeat customer at a game.

TRAILER JOINT – A game housed in a portable trailer. Although less bothersome, compared to the labor of setting up and tearing down Rag joints, it is much more expensive. A Trailer Joint can cost $100 or more per lineal foot, and that is just for the empty shell. The electronics inside have to be bought, and that could drive the price up to $100,000 or more.

WALK IN – A player that comes into a game without being called.

YARD – A hundred dollars.

PLEASE SEND T-SHIRTS TO:

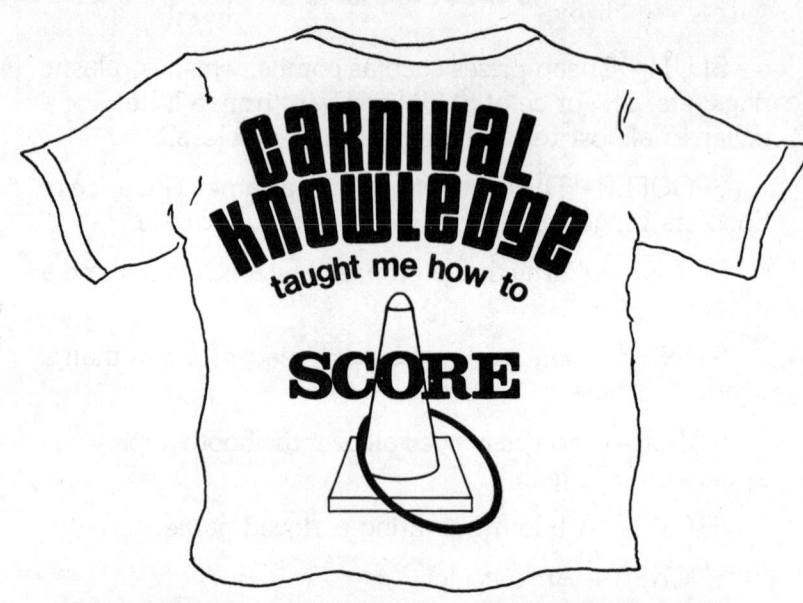

NAME _____

ADDRESS _____

CITY _____ STATE _____ ZIP _____

	RED	BLACK	TAN	AQUA
S				
M				
L				
XL				

Mark the number of shirts you want of each size and color in the appropriate box. Allow 4-6 weeks for delivery.

TOTAL NO. OF SHIRTS	SHP'G AND HNDL'G
1-3	$1.50
4-6	$2.75
over 6	$5.00

Please send me ____ shirts @ $6.95 each $ _____

Shp'g & Hndl'g (see chart)   + _____

Total Enclosed $ _____

SEND CHECK OR MONEY ORDER TO:
SUN PUBLISHING, INC. • DEPT. T-S
1447 PEACHTREE ST. • ATLANTA, GA 30309

THE GAMES

There are seven categories of carnival games: Hanky Pank, Skill, Group, Percentage, Build-Up, Alibi and Flat Store. Here is a little information about each, with tips about some of the more popular games.

HANKY PANK GAMES

A favorite of the younger players, this is the kind of game that usually offers "a prize every time." The only problem is that the prize, more often than not, turns out to be a cheap plastic spider, ring, etc. For this reason these games are referred to as Hanky Panks for, even though a player is assured of winning, the operator uses some Hanky Panky to determine what prize is awarded.

DUCK POND

The Duck Pond has been one of the most popular games on the Midway for decades. For fifty cents the player picks a small wooden or plastic duck floating in a tank of water, hoping his choice is the "Lucky Duck" that wins a big stuffed animal. Most Duck Ponds have either an S, M, or L stamped on the bottom of each duck, representing what size prize the player has won. If an S is picked, the

small prize is a piece of Slum such as a whistle or a comb, costing the Carny maybe a nickle. An M offers a somewhat nicer prize such as a small stuffed snake. A medium prize puts the operator out about fifteen cents. An L offers the player his "choice of the stand" which will usually be a large stuffed animal. Such a prize is worth about two dollars to the operator. Sound like fun? It is, that is if the player doesn't mind getting a cheap plastic comb, for the chances of winning the bright-colored stuffed snake are almost nil, and getting the large stuffed animal is little more than a mirage.

You see, of the large group of little quackers circulating in the tank, there might be two that issue a medium prize. And the Lucky Duck with the L on his belly? Well, an investigator wondered the same thing at a fair in Oklahoma one time and, after his third visit, he decided the little rascal was just too elusive and closed the stand. It seems each time he asked the operator to pluck an L from the water, the lone winner had somehow been removed from the tank.

Leaving the "winner" on the floor or in the change apron are two ways to keep the big prizes gathering dust, but they also present a problem when a quick L has to be produced. The easiest way operators avoid not only problems, but choice winners, is to attach a Lucky Duck with a magnet on its belly to the inside of the tank top. (See Diagram.) This way, if questioned, the operator simply sticks a hand through one of the holes, pretending to shove the ducks toward the front, while plucking off the winner.

Some concessionaires shy away from such shady methods and always give a player an honest chance at each prize displayed. Even if the prize is a cheap ring, that ring in a variety store would probably cost about the price of the game, and to the little player it is just as cherished as the bear because the little tyke won it himself.

TAG BALLOON

"Bust one, you win," comes the call of the operator. And for fifty cents a player can do just that. Behind each balloon is a tag reading S, M, or L, again standing for a small, medium, or large prize, but once again the big winner can turn out to be as elusive as the Duck. When asked to prove there's a winner, the clerk takes a dart from his change apron (along with an L tag) and pops a few balloons. When the tags are removed from the board, the palmed L tag is added to the group and bingo! If only the player had hit *that* balloon! After the player is convinced, the S tags are returned to the board and the dart, along with the L tag winner, is put back into the apron. Another way to avoid a choice winner is to leave the L tag behind a balloon that has already been broken, or place it in a position that is shielded from the player.

PITCH 'TIL YOU WIN

Another favorite of the younger player, this game consists of tossing six-inch wooden hoops at rows of various sized targets. If a small peg is ringed, the player is awarded whatever piece of Slum is on it. The large blocks may offer certain prizes such as radios, watches, cash or the player's choice. The player continues throwing until a target is circled, but be ready for another cheap plastic comb, for a ring can only get around a choice block by going on from the back first. Of course, rebounds don't count! This is still a lot of fun for the little guys, even if the prize is only a toy spider, etc.

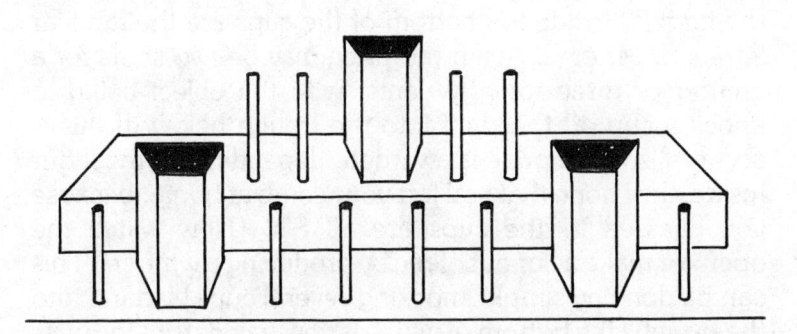

CORK GALLERY

A player purchases a certain number of cork stoppers—two for a quarter, three for a half-dollar, or whatever. The corks are placed into the end of an air rifle. The player takes aim and shoots at various targets. Annie Oakley could have had trouble with this one, but it's fun trying. There are several variations.

CIGARETTE JOINT: The player takes aim with the cork gun at either real or candy cigarette packs, or at boxes of matches. Not a genuine "prize every time" game, the player is awarded whatever prize he knocks off the four-inch shelf. Of course, the real cigarettes are the prime target and therefore the clerk places them closer to the front so a direct hit will usually do little more than lay them down. Too bad, for to win the prize, the pack must be knocked completely off! To further entice the player, a pack of cigarettes will be placed inside a plastic case with a dollar and sometimes a five dollar bill wrapped around it. If you think winning a simple pack of smokes is hard, just wait until you tackle this baby, for the added weight of the case and bill sends a cork ricochetting like a speeding bullet off the chest of Superman!

CUP JOINT: Paper cups are lined up on the shelves as the targets. Inside the bottom of the cups are the familiar letters S, M, or L. Again the price may be two shots for a quarter or three for fifty cents, with the object being to knock a cup off the shelf into the trough below. If this is accomplished, a prize is awarded, depending on the letter inside. Just hope that you left your comb at home, because you guessed it, the cups are all S's! (Now watch the operator make a liar out of me by producing a winner.) This can be done by simply knocking several cups by hand into the trough (the bottom of which is concealed from the view of the player), and switching one of the S's for an M or L that is already in the trough just for that purpose.

TARGET JOINT: The shots and price are the same, but the idea is simply to knock over a wooden target shaped like an L. The prize values are based on the S, M, or L marked on the bottom. The base, which is hidden from the player, gets longer with the quality of the prize. Thus, the

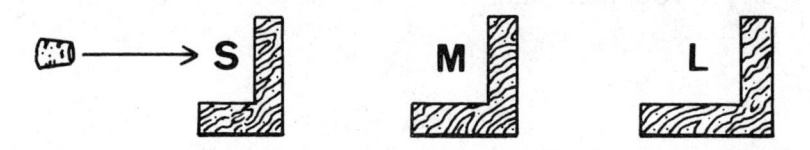

short base of the S can be knocked over easily but the longer base of the M is much more difficult, and the long base of the L can't be tipped even with a direct hit! Toy spider or comb again!

PING-PONG BALLS: Once again, for the same price as above, the player takes aim, but this time the target is a ping-pong ball resting on the mouth of a coke bottle. When a ball is hit, it falls into a trough. You guessed it – all the M's and L's are in the trough!

So, regardless of which type of Cork Gallery is played, you probably won't win very much but it's great fun acting like Dan'l Boone. Who knows, it might even save a romance. After all, no girl likes a fella with uncombed hair!

Note: The fact that the best prize to be expected is a cheap piece of Slum does not mean that the operator has no scruples. You win your comb fair and square, without the rifle sight being tampered with!

APPLE DART

A player purchases a dart and takes aim at a board filled with colored decals of apples. A hit in the red body of the fruit is rewarded with a piece of Slum, and a hit in the much smaller green stem wins a nicer prize, such as a medium snake. How do you win the teddy bears on display? You play until you can trade in three snakes, dummy!

POSTER JOINT

One of the best bets for a prize compatible with the investment of your money. A player pays fifty cents for a dart and tries to hit one of the colorful posters tacked to a board. Of course there is space between the targets, which results in a loss, but there are also plenty of posters. Although the prize costs the operator less than a dime, the same poster can cost close to a dollar in a store, so shoot away! Oh, there is one thing – the nicer felt posters scattered throughout the stand can only be obtained by trading in two of the others which, of course, you must win first.

SLUM SPINDLE

A round board with pie-like sections is placed flat on the counter. Each section reads either Small, Medium, or Large. The L sections are not only scarce, but much narrower. Sometimes the S sections will be filled with Slum. The board has an arrow attached to its center. The idea is to spin the arrow and hope the plastic tip winds up in an L section. The chances of this happening are about the same as hitting the Irish Sweepstakes because the metal prongs dividing the sections are deceivingly different. While the arrow is spinning, the operator has a hidden device that is activated by pressing against it with his stomach. This motion raises the arrow slightly, not enough to be detected, but enough to end the game in an S section.

STAR JOINT

Three darts can be bought for fifty cents and the player must hit the sparsely scattered decals on a board. The decals are half-inch colored stars which determine the size of the prize awarded. Example: Three hits out of three throws wins the player's choice, which is usually a stuffed animal costing the operator about six bucks. This is not bad when you consider that the same prize would cost over twenty in a store. Two hits out of three usually gets something like a snake. And one hit? Well, if you need to spruce up, a comb always comes in handy.

MIRROR JOINT

For fifty cents a dart, if you hit a two-inch star, a mirror is the prize. A good game.

ROLL DOWN

The idea is to roll six rubber balls down an inclined board into numbered slots ranging from one to six. A total score of 6, 7, 8, 9, 10, 32, 33, 34, 35, or 36 produces a choice winner. An 11, 12, 13, 14, 15, 27, 28, 29, 30, or 31 wins a medium prize. Anything between wins a small prize – you guessed it – a comb. The only problem is that the slots giving a 1, 2, 5, and 6 are slanted in just slightly at the top, so when the balls make contact with the slanted opening, they usually rebound over to the wider openings of 3 and 4. And just by coincidence, a bunch of 3's and 4's usually add up to a score worth a small prize!

Caution: Even with such odds, this game can only be considered a Hanky Pank if all six balls are rolled separately. If the operator ever gives you the option of rolling all of the balls at once, it becomes an Alibi or Flat Store game.

SKILL GAMES

By far the best bet on the Midway is this group of games, not only because the result is determined largely by the skill of the participant, but also because better quality prizes are awarded.

BOZO

"I can't believe it!" comes the high-pitched voice from inside the cage. "Did any of your momma's children live?" Such cat-calls are what makes this attraction one of the most enjoyable games to be found on any Midway. The player throws balls at a target protruding from the cage; a good hit sends the heckler into the tank of water below. This is one of the all-time favorites. So regardless of the rumor that a hidden device controls the target and cage, my advice is to invest a buck and dunk the sucker!

LONG RANGE SHOOTING GALLERY

There is no prize for this game, but it is an enjoyable experience. A good shot can be proud of his marksmanship. So lay down a buck and pick up a rifle! Some say that there are crooked sights and hidden devices to keep the targets from falling! Don't listen to such babbling! Ready on the right... ready on the left... ready...

HI-STRIKER

This is the famous test of strength, where a player takes a hammer and tries to send a metal cylinder sliding up the wire track to the top. The last thing a Carny needs is a rigged Hi-Striker. In fact, the ringing bell at the top is music to the operator's ears, for this makes all the by-standers more confident, and they too will want to play. When the bell is rung, the prize is a cigar or straw hat that costs the Carny about a nickel. So even if every player turned out to be a he-man, the operator could care less. He'll sell nickle cigars for half a buck all day long!

LADDER CLIMB

Like a Bozo or Hi-Striker, this is not only a fun game to play but to watch as well. The idea is to climb an angled ladder and ring the bell at the top. Accomplish this, and a nice prize is awarded.

Here's the catch. The ladder is attached at both ends by a swivel hook which makes climbing about as easy as reaching the top of a well-greased pole. You may fall, but don't worry, for the huge air pillow below makes sure that the only damage will be to your pride. Go ahead, mountain climber, the peak can be reached. Just take your time and concentrate!

MACHINE GUNS

For fifty cents the player fires a 100 BB's from a replica machine gun at a target. Shoot the red star out and a teddy bear is awarded. This is a fair and enjoyable game. But take my advice and shoot slowly, cutting around the outside of the red because, remember, all the red must be out!

LONG RANGE FOOTBALL

Plunk down fifty cents and act like Joe Namath! If you can pass a football through a tire twenty feet away, you win! Just make sure you understand what you win, for sometimes the stuffed animal on the wall you expected turns out to be a Rag prize from under the counter.

LONG RANGE BASKETBALL

If you sink two-for-two regulation basketballs through a regulation hoop, from a regulation distance of a free throw, you can win a nice teddy bear. A Carny that rigs this type of game must have sawdust in his brain. The game is hard enough as it is, and an occasional winner is well worth the prize, because a winner draws more players. Nevertheless some operators resort to such tactics as over-inflating balls and wrapping tape around the rim. The infamous trick that landed a Carny in jail was making the hoop two inches smaller than the ball!

TIP OVER BOTTLE

For fifty cents the player gets one shot at tipping over two bottles. This may sound easy, but the small rubber ball must be thrown underhanded. It can be done; but patience, concentration, and perfect aim are needed to win a teddy bear.

PUNK RACK

The player purchases three baseballs for fifty cents and throws at the rows of small stuffed cats. If you knock over three out of three cats, you win a bear; it's that simple. Not two out of three, or one out of three, but three out of three.

BREAK A PLATE/RECORD

One throw is all you get for fifty cents. If you break or chip two of the closely racked plates or records, you win a stuffed toy. If the feat isn't accomplished, blame your arm, for there is nothing wrong with the target!

BREAK A BOTTLE

Okay, Sandy Koufax, you've got one shot to rear back and show your stuff. Don't worry about the beer bottle you're trying to break; it's legit. If you miss, what the heck. Everyone has an off day. The fifty cents was a reasonable investment for a chance at a teddy bear and some clean fun.

BEAN BAG

A player is given two bean bags for fifty cents to throw at six coke cans stacked in a pyramid. If the cans are knocked from their stand, the player wins a good prize. It's fun, but they all must be spilled.

FISH UP BOTTLE

Any fisherman can tell you the frustration of the "one that got away," and any player of this game can well sympathize with this plight.

Here he takes a fishing pole with a small plastic ring at the end of the line. The object? To loop the ring around the neck of a beer bottle which is lying on its side and bring it to a standing position. Make it stand and you may win a prize even better than a teddy bear. But let it fall and you join the ranks of frustrated fishermen.

It's a painstakingly slow procedure, but give it a try. It's only fifty cents!

SKEE BALL

You get eight balls to roll down a lane into numbered circles. The numbers vary from ten to fifty and a prize is awarded based on your total score.

The larger the number, the smaller the circle. Hence, it's difficult to get a high score. So take your time and concentrate! The price is right— eight balls for a dime. But the bargain can be deceiving, for it takes quite a few dimes to get a decent prize.

ONE BALL

This is the most controversial skill game in the business. Why? Because the majority of One Balls are worked in a shady fashion. Even if the game is worked legitimately, it is no easy task to win. Just think about it. The player has one try to take a softball and spill three 3-pound wooden bottles from their stand. If the throw is weak or the hit is a fraction off-center, the player can forget it.

If the game is worked legitimately, the bottles are lined flush, and are of equal weight.

If not, one of the bottles is much heavier and placed slightly to the rear. Since the bottles are placed in a pyramid, and the heavy bottle is on the bottom and to the back, a good hit will catch the lighter bottles first, expending some of the velocity needed to knock over the heavy one. To show it can be done, the operator places the heavy bottle on top and throws. The ball spills the two light bottles and the momentum carries the weighted one off. It looks so easy when *he* does it!!

GROUP GAMES

These are games where more than one player is involved in the competition. The majority of these games are legitimate but, unfortunately, they are also termed illegal under the gambling statutes of most states. The law states that a game constitutes gambling if a wager is placed, where anything of value is returned, and the player's skill has no control over the outcome of the game.

In my opinion, such a law should not pertain to carnivals, for not only do such games offer the lucky winner a nice prize for the wager, but the excitement of the competition is worth the price of the game.

MOUSE GAME

Some group games can be rigged, and this is one of them. The set-up involves a live mouse inside an "arena" whose sides have numbered holes. The object is to place a wager on the number of the hole which the player thinks the rodent will enter. The prize awarded can either be a stuffed toy or cash, depending on how the carnival has been fixed.

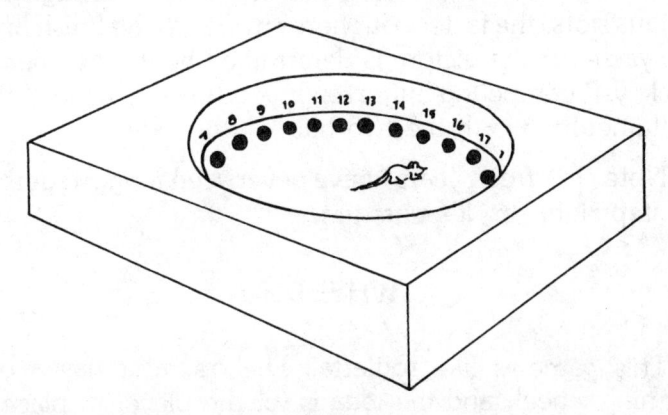

In the diagram above, the mouse is about to enter hole number 17. If a player had placed a quarter on that number, he would win a stuffed animal worth about $1.50 to the Carny. The game offers three counters with sixteen wagering spots on each. If all the counters are full, there must be at least three winners each game. Since more than one person can bet on the same space, sometimes the wagers are heavy on a certain number. When this happens, especially when the game is played for money, the need arises for the operator to help the mouse "make up its mind." How? He takes his handkerchief, which he uses for an occasional cough, dips the cloth into a hidden dish of ammonia and, as he spins the wheel, rubs the scent around the hole with the least number of bets. To the mouse, the smell of ammonia resembles that of cheese so when the mouse is released, guess where it goes!

DERBY

Place your bets, 'cause it's off to the races! It costs a quarter to pick a nag and help him to the finish line. This game is a pin-ball like device. The player works a spring lever. The faster you return the ball racing through the various slots, the faster your horse moves to the finish line. The prize for the victory is determined by the number of "jockeys" competing but, even if you finish dead last, the excitement is worth the two bits.

Note: In fifteen years I have never seen a rigged derby. So step right up, it's post time!

WHEEL

This game is like roulette. The operator has a big spinning wheel, and the idea is for the player to place a wager on the space where he thinks the wheel arrow will stop. If he wins, he gets a stuffed animal comparable to the one issued in the mouse game.

BINGO

Is there anyone who doesn't know this universal game? It's a sad thing, but this is another so-called gambling game, even though it is one of the few enjoyments for the elderly fairgoer. I never could understand why Bingo can be played in the basement of a church for money and not on a Midway for merchandise! Still, this is an unrigged and fun game.

I GOT IT

A game similar to Bingo. The idea is to toss rubber balls into a tray filled with holes. The first player to line three in a row yells, "I got it!" and wins the game. The balls are thrown one at a time at the command of the caller. The prize offered is once again determined by the number of players. If a winner desires a particular prize, he or she can be issued a coupon and, after a few more wins, the electric blanket on the top shelf is attainable.

Many times when Bingo is excluded from the Midway, the steady ring of "I got it" can still be heard. And why not? This fun game appeals to all ages and, even with a minimum number of competitors, the prize is well worth the quarter investment.

HUFF 'N PUFF

Similar to a Derby, the outcome of the race depends on the skill of each player in handling the plunger before him. The faster the plunger, the faster the horse or dog races to victory. Once again the prize is determined by the number of racers. So, when you see such a game, step up and invest a quarter. Who knows? You might be the one to win "choice of the stand!"

WATER RACE

Plunk down a quarter, pick out a water pistol, and take aim at the clown's mouth before you. When the game starts, the amount of water which you shoot into it will determine how fast you will fill the balloon on top of the clown's head. The first player to burst his balloon is the winner. The more players, the bigger the prize!

Nothing but fun and in no way rigged! The only problem with this game is the smart bimbo who just can't resist turning the water pistol on the operator. This is not only senseless and rude, but dangerous as well. The operator is surrounded by electrical current and that combined with water could result in a fatal shock.

Many fights have resulted between Carnies and Marks over such pranks. If you ever see this occur, go for a cop, because such a stunt can be dangerous to all participants.

CRAZY BALL

Lay a quarter on one of the colored spots on the counter. If the ball being tossed into the center tray lands on the same color, you win a stuffed animal with a retail of about forty times the investment! I have repeatedly stated that Crazy Ball is one of the best bets on any Midway to win a decent prize.

A player is picked at random to toss the ball, and the numbered holes in the tray are in plain sight. This is a fun game that offers a player an exciting, fair chance to take a nice souvenir home!

I've spoken in defense of this game many times. Certainly it can be "gambling," but such betting is what attracts millions to carnival games each year. So if you see this game, I strongly urge you to play it!

PERCENTAGE GAMES

These are games where the Carny depends on a volume of business for a profit. Some percentage games can be summed up as flat out gambling, where the transaction is cash for cash. Many others are just as innocent as any Group game. These games are difficult to play but offer the best chances of winning a giant stuffed animal on any Midway.

DIGGERS

We might as well start with the game that has drawn more criticism than any other. The Digger, or Steam Shovel, as it is sometimes called, is not a rigged game! I do admit that at one time these simple games were some of the most dangerous to be found on a carnival lot. That was when the prizes below the searching claw were valuable items such as silver dollars and twenty-dollar gold pieces. Today's Digger offers prizes such as Slum, pocket knives, and cigarette lighters. If scooped up, this kind of prize offers the player something worth, at the most, fifty cents to the Carny.

The toy crane has a set of gears which prevents the arm from backing up, but this does not mean that the game is rigged. The purpose of this mechanism is not to cheat, but rather to speed up the game. You must remember that the profits from this type of game depend on the volume of customers and, if a player were allowed to go at his own rate, the machine might be tied up for an hour or so for, at the most, a quarter.

No, the cranes aren't rigged. But if you don't believe me, just ask the Carny kids on any Midway. The game is one of their favorites. And why not? They win more choice prizes than they know what to do with!

PENNY FALL/BULLDOZER

In this game, the player pays a quarter to activate a sweeping arm that pushes quarters or tokens toward a ledge. The player is rewarded by receiving the ones pushed over the edge. It's tantalizing because the player believes that, if he spends just one more quarter, the huge stack of coins teetering on the edge will be returned to him.

Fat chance. That is part of the deception. You see, those particular stacks are carefully arranged by the operator so that their weight will force the other stack into slots which return nothing to the player.

Most Carnies frown on the appearance of Penny Falls on a Midway for they know that, as they put it, the games "suck up every quarter on the lot."

The Bulldozer is the same game but, instead of by an arm, the coins are pushed by a toy bulldozer. Although these games, when they first were introduced, were rigged, there are current variations that are honest and should be allowed.

You can spot an honest Penny Fall by looking for these important differences. When the game operates for merchandise or when tokens replace the quarters inside the game, the element of gambling is greatly reduced because the player does not play for money. To further reduce the element of chance, the player is offered two additional means of enhancing his odds. One is a moveable chute which allows the player to aim the tokens and thus place them where he wants them to go (if he has good aim). More importantly, a button has been added that allows the player to stop the arm (usually a windshield wiper) whenever he wants so he can build the tokens in the desired area. When I actually demonstrated that such a game worked this way I placed 19 out of 21 tokens in the place I predetermined, so I could win.

It needs to be emphasized that all of this type of game should not be eliminated. The investment for Carnies is great ($25,000 or more), and they have gone to much trouble to revamp the games so that players can win. The Carny wants to be able to use these games, and if the *honest* ones are closed by misinformed game inspectors, the Carny is the loser.

DICE TABLE

Sounds like gambling? It is, because the player places a wager on the throw of the dice. He can bet that the dice will land over seven, under seven, or hit seven on the head. Example: If a player lays a dollar on "under seven" and the dice come up six, he is paid his dollar plus one from the dealer. The same process occurs if a winner bets "over" and wins. If the gambler wants to be a high roller, he can bet on seven, which returns his wager plus double that amount from the dealer. Ah, what's a little innocent gambling at the county fair?

CHECKERBOARD DART

A large board covered with red and white squares outlined in black is placed at the back of a booth. The players are given the opportunity to place wagers on the red, black, or white squares on one of the three counters. After all bet are down, the dealer picks a random player who throws a dart into the board. Red or white pays one for one, and those daring to bet on the thin black lines are rewarded three for one. Nothing to it, just plunk down whatever amount you feel comfortable with, and let lady luck do her thing!

SPOT PITCH

The player throws dimes onto a large flat board on which are scattered small red dots or Lucky Strike cigarette decals. If he gets a dime perfectly within a dot or box, he gets a very good prize that may be worth up to $75.00 in a retail store.

Note: I have heard of this game being rigged with greased boards and layers of shellac to make it impossible for a coin to stay on the target. This is unfounded. Certainly the boards are kept waxed, but the reason is to protect the expensive wood from the elements. The shellac gives the board a nicer appearance – at least the Carnies think so. That's the reason they use it.

The next time you see a player walking around with a huge stuffed animal, ask him where he won it. The chances are good that he'll tell you by tossing dimes on red dots at the Spot Pitch booth.

GOBLET/GLASS PITCH

Buy a buck's worth of ping-pong balls and try to arc them in a way so that they stay in the glass or plate of your choice. What you hit is what you get. Sometimes instead of ping-pong balls, the player tosses either nickels or dimes, but the end is the same.

Note: Another tale is that the targets are greased. I don't see how this can be true. In all honesty, I've seen many a player at these stands with the real dilemma of how to get his dishes, stacked up under his chin, home safe and sound!

PLATE PITCH

In this game, the player tosses either dimes or quarters at plates resting on the heads of large stuffed animals. If the coin stays on the plate, one of these animals is awarded sometimes costing the Carny twenty bucks. The game is made harder by the amount of space between each animal. The game also is difficult because of the angle from which the player tosses the coin. This is a hard one, but think of an operator having to give away those $20 animals to everyone!

GOLD FISH JOINT

Toss a ping-pong ball into one of the many small bowls, and you win a finny friend. The only thing wrong with this game is that the player is usually under the impression that the attractive bowl comes with the inhabitant. No way; but the operator will keep your new pet until you're ready to leave and then let you carry it away in a little plastic bag.

RING A BOTTLE

A player is given three rings for fifty cents or seven for a dollar. If one of the rings lands around the neck of a bottle, the player is given a giant stuffed animal that costs the operator at least $35. A computer has figured the odds of winning this game are 600-to-one. This may be so but, too many times, I have seen a player invest fifty cents and lug away a life-sized animal. At one fair in Oklahoma, I saw Carnies place wooden stobs in the bottle necks to improve the player's odds. But at the same time they had to offer much smaller prizes to the winners. The point is that, considering the Carny's expenses, the odds for Ring A Bottle are just right – fair for the Carny and fair for the player.

BEAR HOOPLA

Take your pick: three rings for fifty cents or seven for a dollar. Toss the large wooden ring around the stuffed animal tied to the stob – and you lose! You see, the idea is to completely circle the base of the stob. Do this and you win a stuffed animal identical to the one on the stob. Sure, the clearance is close, but there are still a lot of winners.

BUILD UP GAMES

These games are where a player must trade in a prize to achieve a bigger one.

There is nothing wrong with this unless there are no posted rules or the Agent forgets to tell you. In other words, if a player walks up, sees nothing but stuffed animals, plunks down the price of a game, wins, and finds that the prize for a "first" win is the small Rag being pulled from under the counter, he would certainly feel deceived.

That deception is the least of the player's worries. If the game is being run "Coney Island Style," the customer

better hold on to his wallet! A game run this way can milk a player as fast as a Mitt Camp because the Agent is an expert at fast talk. "You made one, sir, I'll make one for you. Make one more and you get a bigger prize. Don't worry about paying me now. I trust you. Pay me when it's over!" The Agent keeps a ball or dart in the player's hand at all times, repeating, "one more, one more, pay me when it's over!" The only problem is that when it's over, the player is shocked to learn that he owes for forty games at fifty cents apiece! If a player pays as he goes, and fully understands what he is paying for, there would be no concern with Build Ups!

BUST THREE BALLOONS

The player purchases three darts for fifty cents and tries to hit the balloons. This sounds simple but, the game is still confusing. There are two sizes of balloons on the board. The majority are normally inflated, but there is a single row of underinflated ones across the top. If this doesn't confuse the player, then the wide variety of prizes should. What do you have to do to win which prize? The fast talking Agent will gloss over such concerns.

Note: If you play this game, be sure you understand what you're playing for, and never wait until you're finished! Pay as you go, and you won't owe anything when you finish.

MINI BASKETBALL/FOOTBALL/DONIKER JOINT

Regardless of whether it might be throwing basketballs through a hoop, footballs through a tire, or rolls of toilet paper through a toilet seat, the targets are close for one reason; to make it easy to "Build You Up"! Be careful and go slowly!

PUNK RACK

Unfortunately this "skill" game is sometimes worked as a "You made one, I'll make one for you" scam. If you hear this and want to show off your arm, go find a Break a Bottle or Bozo instead.

ALIBI GAMES

Alibi games are rigged games. When they don't go as planned, the Agent uses an excuse to avoid issuing a choice prize. If you've ever heard a consoling, "Sorry pal, but you went over the foul line," the chances are that you were the victim of an Alibi Game. The Agent is always ready with an "Alibi" if need be.

Although there are more sophisticated rigged games, there are none as suspicious. If you don't believe me, just ask the investigative reporter who lost a $130 in about ten minutes on one of these games at a state fair, or the State Senator who witnessed four young girls, of whom the youngest was eight, lose a bundle in a matter of minutes!

NAIL JOINT

A favorite for players in the building trade, the idea is to take a hammer and with three single hits, drive and seat three nails into a railroad tie.

How can a professional carpenter miss? It's easy. You see, inside the operator's change apron special nails are kept.

The nails must be driven completely into the tie to win. If any one of the three nails are bent, the player loses. So the operator has at least one nail that is soft in the middle. You can guess the result.

BUSHEL BASKET

This is the most common Alibi game. The idea is for the player to toss softballs into a Bushel Basket. The rules are simple: if the balls stay in, the player wins. If they bounce out, the player loses.

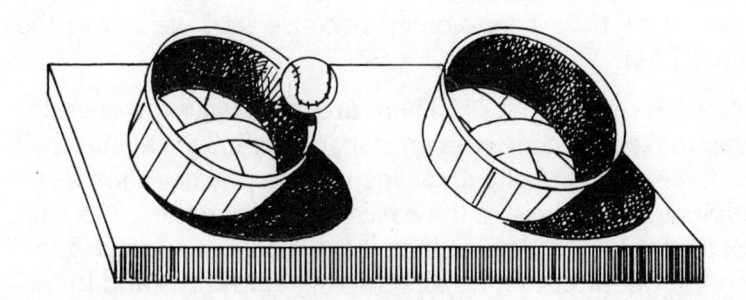

The player is usually enticed to play by the offer of a free practice shot. The problem is that the operator demonstrates how easy it is by lobbing the ball into the basket from inside the booth at a considerably shorter distance than the distance for the potential customer. From this short distance the ball will stay in the basket. Then the operator will allow a free practice shot. The majority of the time the player will be amazed at how easy he can make his free practice shot – and equally amazed at how easily the ball bounces out once he has paid.

How can this happen? After the operator tosses the ball from the shorter distance, he leaves it in the basket in order to kill the bounce which causes the ball to rebound out. The basket is "dead," and the free practice ball tossed by the player from the longer distance will stay inside. But once the money is collected both balls are removed and, from the distance of the player, the balls will bounce out.

There are two very important Alibies used with this game. One involves the RED RIM. Sometimes the steady bouncing of balls against the flimsy slate of the basket will crack or deaden the basket and the balls will stay in. When this happens the operator uses the Alibi that the player hit the red painted rim around the outside of the basket, and of course the sign posted conveniently states that rim shots don't count. The other involves the FOUL LINE: You'd be surprised at how many winners are shocked to find out their wins have been voided because they went over the Foul Line.

FOR INSPECTION: There are three ways the operator can make this game pass an inspection: 1) by leaving a ball in the basket and giving the inspector a practice shot; 2) by changing the angle of the basket (the lower the bottom lip of the basket, the less chance there is of the ball staying in – so the operator merely tilts the angle upwards and therefore makes a practice try much easier); 3) by allowing the inspector to toss heavier balls (the lighter the weight of the balls, the better chance of the ball bouncing out – so many times the balls used for inspection are water logged. With these balls you get a nod of approval from the inspector who just sank eight out of ten shots!)

If you like to toss softballs, I suggest you join a league and stay away from this game. There have been arrests and convictions on this game in Oklahoma!

FLUKEY BALL

The idea is to take a plastic baseball and toss it underhanded against a slightly slanted board. This board will have some kind of target on it (frequently a clown's face). To be a winner, a player must hit the target so the ball will rebound into the plastic garbage can sitting below.

The tape around the baseball is very important to this game because it conceals a cut in the ball. Such a cut alone can deaden a ball but sometimes the cut is made so the operator can fill the ball with cotton, graphite, or some similar light substance. The garbage can is situated to catch all tampered balls, but untampered ones will rebound wide because they have more bounce. How can you lose? Inside the can, hidden under a towel, is an untampered ball. The operator can make a player hit or miss the shot by simply switching the balls.

Note: At a state fair in Kentucky a few years back, this game was closed. When the State Police got wise and jumped the counter, they found two balls inside the can and discovered that one had been tampered with. You can guess the rest.

PUSH UP/PULL UP BOTTLE

How simple can it be? All you have to do is place the end of a two-pronged fork under the neck of the bottle and ease it up to a standing position. The bottle, tilted into the V-cut of a stand, is positioned in such a way that if the player eases it up either too fast or too hard the bottle will tip over, and the player loses. If he is slow and easy the bottle will stand upright on the small platform, and he will be a winner.

At least that's the way the game operator explains it, but nothing could be farther from the truth.

The trick is not in the way the bottle is eased up at all but rather in the way the bottle is "set." You see, most bottle bottoms are heavier on one side than the other. So if the operator places the heavy part toward the front, the bottle will stand. But if the added weight is to the rear, the bottle will fall. For the operator to control this action, it is important for the platform base to be perfectly level.

What happens if the player gets wise and wants to position his own bottle? Under the back leg of the platform is a ruler which is carefully hidden by the covering. If the ruler is removed, the board is no longer level – not enough to be easily detected, but enough to make the bottle spill over no matter how the bottle is set. So if a player becomes wise to the uneven weight in the bottle's bottom or to the way the bottle is positioned, the operator simply picks up the platform and bottle and shows that there is nothing to the game but a simple board and bottle. The two are replaced but, unknown to the player, this time the back stand is resting off the ruler, assuring that the player will lose.

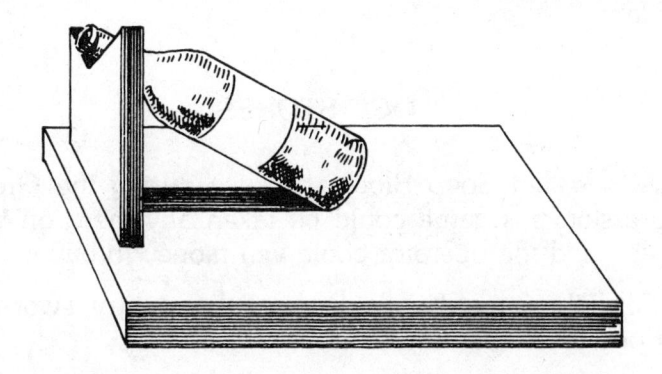

Although most 6½ to 10-ounce bottles will work, the operator is careful to shy away from a bottle with a label or colored markings. The reason for this is that such lettering might be enough to tip off a skeptical eye that the bottle is being turned as it is set down.

A variation of this game is called Pull Up Bottle. The set-up and rules are the same, but instead of the player pushing up the bottle with a fork, the bottle is pulled up with a small cane.

Note: Sometimes instead of relying on a piece of ruler, the operator will use well concealed holes in the counter. The platform rests on screws which conveniently fit into the holes. If the operator slightly moves the platform so that one screw is out of the hole, once again the platform is no longer level.

FOR INSPECTION: Let the operator show the game, look at the difference in the thickness of the glass in the bottom of the bottle, feel for the ruler or the holes, and close the game.

The following Alibi games are similar to the previous ones, and the alibis and inspection techniques are also similar.

BLOCK STORES

Also called Soup Blocks because during the Great Depression this game could be taken anywhere on the streets, and the operator could win money to buy soup.

Of all the games I worked around the country, I worked this one more than any other.

A player is given three rings to toss and completely loop around a block. The rules are quite simple. The player receives three 4-inch rings for a dollar. Ringing one out of three wins a small prize worth a nickel or so, such as a whistle. Two out of three wins a medium prize which is a stuffed animal in the $1.50 to $2.00 range, and three out of three entitles the player to the choice of the stand.

The operator has a standard spiel to entice a player into the game. "If I helped you win a choice prize, you would tell your friends where you won it, wouldn't you? I'll tell you what. Put up a dollar and ring just one and, instead of giving you a small prize, I'll let you pick out your choice!"

Such a deal sounds inviting but, little does the player know, the block is cut so that out of a hundred tosses the average player would get a hundred misses. Oh, the ring will fit around the block all right – but just barely (see figure A).

An average block is cut at angles with the highest point to the rear measuring 4¼ inches from the top to bottom. From this height it drops to a height of 3 inches at the front. The block measures 2½ inches across. The reason for the difficulty in properly ringing it lies in the slant running from front to rear, which measures 3½ inches. With such a clearance, the ring can be dropped from a distance of six inches directly above the block and the ring would not fit. True, the ring will go half way on (figure B), but another posted sign states that this is the wrong way and, of course, means a loser.

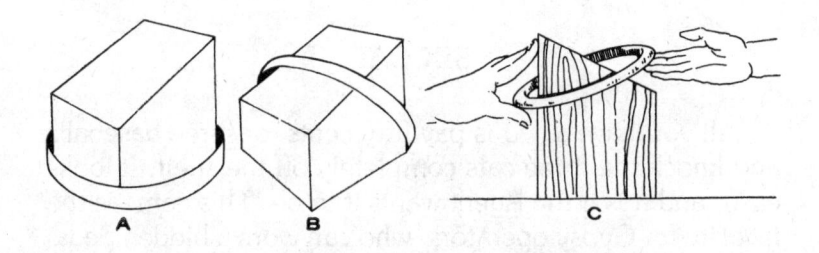

The only way the tossed ring will totally encircle the block is for it to go on from the back first. Of course, there is another sign voiding rebounds.

The operator, in an attempt to show the player how simple it is, moves the block closer until finally the block is placed on the front counter. The player is allowed to place the ring on the tips of his straightened fingers and push it over the top of the block.

The operator steadies the player's hand while the operator places his own thumb and finger behind the block.

As the ring clears the top, the operator's finger and thumb stop the ring, and thus the player thinks he has accomplished the feat needed to win. The operator can do this every time because of many hours of continuous practice. Such practice is needed to conceal the fact that as the ring eases over the back corners of the block the operator is in fact hooking it with a move of his wrist and finger tips. Of course, when the player tries it for real, the operator's help is missing from the back of the block, and either the ring will fall or wind up going half on (figure C). The player is enticed to keep trying when the operator moves the block closer. But when this happens the ante goes up.

FOR INSPECTION: Many times the operator will replace the standard 4-inch rings with some much larger in order to pass inspection. Of course this is just a temporary arrangement.

SIX CAT

All you have to do is pay fifty cents for three baseballs and knock the three cats completely off the shelf. It looks easy, and it is if the Agent wants it to be. This game is the favorite for Gypsy operators, who can work a hidden pedal under the counter.

The rigging is concealed by Flash Cloth and the construction of the booth. The pedal engages a rod which runs along the side of the game to the back of the cats. When the Agent pushes down on the pedal, the rod engages a slot which moves forward and catches the falling cat, preventing it from falling off the shelf. What can I say? Don't play this one!

OVER THE RAIL BUCKET

This game is housed in a wooden box that usually sits on the game counter. The player rolls a ball down an incline trying to bounce it from the first section over a wooden rail and into the second section. The trick is that, underneath the false bottom of the game box, there is a spring-like device which allows the operator to demonstrate how easy his game is. The Agent rolls a ball, it hits in the first section and bounces over the rail, but the Agent catches it *before* it strikes the bottom of the second section. The player is then given a trial shot and it is always successful. As a matter of fact, as long as the ball is not allowed to hit the back section, the ball will always bounce over the rail to the back section. But once the ball hits in the back section, the hidden device seesaws its weight to make the front section "dead." The next ball hitting the front section will have no bounce and will not even clear the rail!

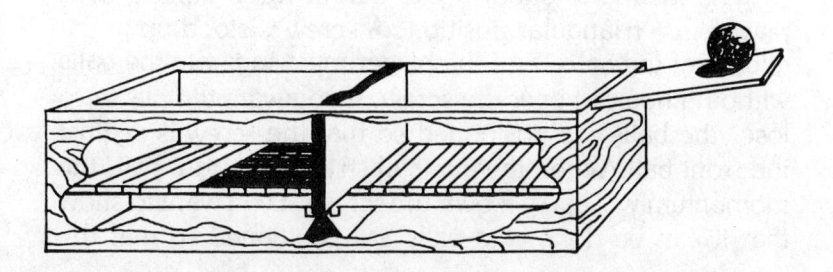

ENGLISH POOL

The player hits a cue ball, trying to knock a half dollar, resting on another ball, out of a circle. If the coin is centered directly on top of the ball (figure A) it will land in the circle, thus the player loses. If the Agent wants to show that it can be done, he simply sets the coin slightly off-center on top of the ball (figure B), and the momentum of the striking ball will carry the coin out of the circle. Another way of controlling this game is to use two cue balls. One is larger than the other and will knock out the coin. Hence, the operator uses that ball. At the end of the playing surface is a trough, the bottom of which is concealed from the player. A nice way to switch balls, wouldn't you say?

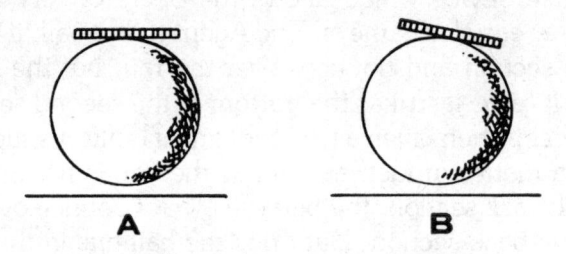

A   **B**

THREE BALL POOL

The idea is to shoot a cue ball at three billiard balls placed in a triangular position. A screw is stood up in the middle of the balls, and the player must separate the balls without knocking over the screw. If you want the player to lose, the balls are positioned so that the screw is against the front ball. When the cue ball strikes the front ball, the momentum will carry it over the screw. If you want to show that it can be done, the balls are positioned so that the screw rests between the two back balls, thus the striking balls will separate without disturbing the screw.

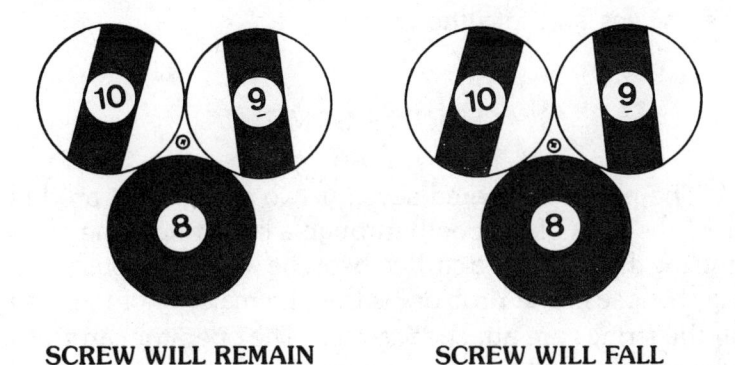

SCREW WILL REMAIN **SCREW WILL FALL**

BIG TOM

A single, large, two-faced stuffed cat is placed on a shelf to the rear of the game booth. This shelf is positioned at eye-level for an average man. The height is important and so is the small upright strip of wood running along the shelf which hides the base of the cat.

The idea of the game is for the player to throw a baseball and spill the cat completely from the shelf and into the trough below. If the cat is simply knocked over, the player loses.

How is this game rigged? Behind the cat and concealed from the view of the player, is another shelf of the same height. It is set at a certain prescribed distance behind the front shelf to form a slot through which the cat could fall – if the Agent wants it to. The base of the cat is much wider on one side. So if the operator wants the cat just to fall over, he places the wider base toward the back. In this position, the striking ball will carry the cat back against the hidden shelf and thus only lay it over. If he wants to show how it can be done, he sets the cat up with its narrow base to the rear. The narrower base will allow the spilled cat to fall between the shelves and into the trough.

STRING GAME

The player is offered seventy-two strings that are fed from the back of the booth through a large ring. If he picks a string that pulls up a stuffed bear, he wins. If he pulls up a tag, he loses. The problem is that the majority of the time *all* the strings are attached to tags. The operator can show a winner at will because under the counter is a pedal running directly to the bear. He pretends to pull a string while he pushes down on the pedal and automatically a bear pops up!

This game is extremely frustrating when the operator drops the odds against the player. He may tell the player to pick out three strings, and that if he pulls up a bear he will receive a cash bonus, the prize and all of his money back. Believe me, this is quite appealing when the customer sees the operator demonstrate how probable a winner is when he *seems* to pull three strings and produces two tags and a winner. (Undetected, the operator actually pulls only two tag strings and uses the pedal to produce the winner.) You can imagine what a temptation it is if you think your odds of winning are down to one out of three!

Another way the operator can show a winner is by actually having one or more strings attached to bears, but double-looping them through the ring. He knows which ones bears are attached to and merely traces the string behind the ring and gives it a tug, making the bear pop up. The player still has no chance of winning because with the string double-looped around the ring it will not pull correctly and the operator will simply explain that the string is broken.

Although the majority of these games are rigged, there are some that are run legitimately. But even if the game is run straight, the best odds the player will be afforded is three winning strings out of seventy-two. And then there is always the chance of the hidden pedal.

COVER THE SPOT

Concentration and practice play a very important part in this game – not for the player, but for the operator!

The idea is for the player to drop five discs onto a red circle and completely cover the red. The operator can accomplish the feat briskly and successfully each time, but no matter how slowly or carefully the player goes, there always seems to be some red left showing.

How can this happen? The player is told to drop the discs from a height of approximately six to eight inches. When the operator demonstrates, the player believes that the operator is doing the same. But the fact is that while the operator moves his hands quickly back and forth, he is in fact palming or placing the discs on the circle.

Many times the operator will reduce the odds for the player by placing from one to four of the discs on the circle and inviting the player to try to cover the red with the remaining discs. Of course, when such a favor is offered the ante goes up, and there is still no way for the player to win.

What happens if the operator places four of the discs and the player happens to get lucky on the last one? The operator will charge that the player dropped it from too close to the board, so it won't count, of course!!

SHORT RANGE SHOOTING GALLERY

A player is offered a chance to show his expertise by firing three shots from a .22 rifle into a small target. The target may be a tiny red dot, a small letter "B", etc. But the results are always the same; there will always be some red left on the target. The operator will even offer to gamble a little by allowing extra shots (for a price, of course). And still the player can't win. Why?

Just as in the Machine Gun game, the only way the target can be completely shot away is for the player to cut around it — and that would take a lot of shots. It is impossible to win.

FLAT STORE GAMES

These are the most dangerous games found on a carnival Midway.

The name FLAT STORE is derived from the fact that with this group of games you can "Flat Out" rob a player! These games are worked by the Agents who are really sophisticated. An important aid for the Agents working this type of game is a "Conversion Chart" which enables the Agent to control every step of the fraud.

With the finesse of the Agent and the use of a Conversion Chart the game worker can easily give points, take

them away, give a prize, give a free game, give money, give a "bonus" or an opportunity to win a T.V. or stereo, but more importantly, he can take money.

Flat Stores are broken down into three groups: Count Stores, Peek Stores, and Wheels. Nevertheless, if the game consists of counting marbles, ringing clothes pins, or spinning an arrow, the result is always the same: for the Agent, a profit; and for the player, an expensive lesson.

COUNT STORES

What do eight marbles, four darts, eight six-sided blocks, and eight miniature footballs have in common? They are all variations of Count Stores.

RAZZLE: A game consisting of eight marbles, and a tray containing 143 holes numbered from one to six.

The player dumps the marbles into the tray and the total accumulated is referred to a Conversion Chart for its worth. This game usually requires the player to score 100 yards or more to win, so the player finds himself in the position of playing more than one game. (Only four numbers on the chart give 100 yards: 8, 9, 47, and 48. According to FBI statistics a player could only roll an 8 or 48 once in every twenty-one billion, five hundred thirty-three million, seven hundred eighty-seven thousand, five hundred eighty-three tries, while a 9 or 47 would only occur once every four billion, five hundred thirty-three million, four hundred twenty-eight thousand, nine hundred sixty-five tries!)

The Agent employs a fast-count technique to keep the player in the game by giving points, chances for better prizes and, often, money. The player throws the marbles into the game board. The Agent then fast-counts the total – and cheats for the player – to give the player a good number. A good number is determined by the conversion chart. If the player continues to get "good" numbers he will put down more and more money to win the big prize. The numbers are not counted legitimately until the end of the game. At that time, stopping the player from winning a prize after spending his money. At the end of the game the numbers that come up are called correctly, but the conversion chart allows no points (yards) for those numbers that occur most often (which are 22-34).

A typical play at a Razzle will happen like this. First the player is enticed by a free game and is almost assured 50 yards on the free roll. The Agent writes the 50 yards down on a score sheet and marks it paid. The player is asked for a quarter bet for two more chances at the additional 50 yards, and the Agent fast-counts the next roll into a total of 42, worth 20 yards. The player quickly has a total of 70 yards with another roll paid for.

Before the marbles settle into the holes the Agent already knows that the player will receive a total calling for an "H.P." This stands for "house pays" – meaning that the smiling operator will swap him two dollars for a dollar plus a free game. The player will gladly oblige, and as luck has it he manages to roll a total of 41 which is worth 15 yards. Now he has a total of 85 yards, and he does not hesitate to pay another quarter for a try at the 15 yards needed to win the stuffed toy. The player is guaranteed a total of 29 which calls for a bonus.

"Shake my hand" smiles the Agent, whipping out a twenty dollar bill. "Now when you win you get a stuffed dog, a T.V. set, and twenty dollars of the boss's money! Put up two dollars and score the 15 yards or more and you get it all!" If the player comes up with the two bucks the Agent is assured of two things; the player is not afraid of the gamble, and the player will get another H.P.

"I don't believe it! What'd you pay for that last game, two dollars?" He hands the player four dollars. "Remember sir, an H.P. pays you two for one plus one free game. Dump'em in?" (At this point the player is $2.50 ahead of the game with 85 yards and a free game coming.)

Now the player is asked for two dollars, and the next roll is a 29 which (you guessed it) is a bonus. "What's 10% of fifty dollars, sir?" smiles the Agent. "That's right! Now when you win you get fifty bucks for a five dollar bet, and all you need is another 13 yards or more!"

On the next roll the player will be awarded 5 yards, putting him 8 yards short. The next roll is a bonus, which doubles the bet to a hundred bucks for ten. The next roll is a total calling for a prize which is usually a two-dollar teddy bear. The next is a loser such as a 30. The next roll gets another 5 yards, putting him 3 yards shy. The next roll is another bonus. Now it costs twenty dollars to play. The next roll gets another prize. The next roll is another losing total. The next roll gets another bonus.

Now the player gets half of the prizes in the stand, five hundred dollars in cash, plus all his money back – all he needs is 3 lousy yards!

The bad part is that now it costs fifty bucks a roll! The next roll will be a 39 worth 2 yards. Now the player is up to 99 yards, and if he comes up with another fifty bucks you can be assured that the next total will be a 29 or bonus. Now it costs the player a hundred dollars at a chance for a thousand, and if he stays with it, the game will be a steady stream of losing totals, prizes, and bonuses from here on out.

It is important to point out that few players carry this

much money with them, but the friendly Agent will gladly hold the game open while the gambler steps out for more cash.

If this is not enough to shy you away from this game, then here are more statistics you might find interesting: the eight marbles can be rolled in fourteen zillion, three hundred twenty-five trillion, nine hundred eighty-two billion, thirty-five million, seven hundred thirty thousand, five hundred sixty different ways! You might wonder what would happen if a player got smart and told the Carny that *he* wanted to count the numbers. In this case the Carny would have to quickly look at the number thrown and make sure it was a loser. If the player beat the tremendous odds and got a winner, the Carny can "palm" a marble as he counts. Remember, he's had much more practice than you have!

COLOR DART OR SPEED DARTS: The Color Dart is very similar to the Razzle in the way the player is taken.

A dart board is positioned inside the booth with the same sequence of numbers as in the Razzle (11 ones, 19 twos, 39 threes, 44 fours, 19 fives, and 11 sixes). To further complicate the play, the squares housing the numbers are quite small, and the lines are bordered with string. This string not only serves as an effective device to keep the player from receiving the number he actually hits, but more importantly to the Agent, it increases the odds over the Razzle. (A sign posted inside the booth states that all darts striking a line count as three.)

Instead of the player spilling out eight marbles, he throws four darts into a board, either one or two at a time, or all four at once. The player is made to throw the darts 2 or more at a time to speed up the game and to avoid allowing the player to take time to aim precisely at the point he wants. Two of the darts are colored and count triple the number hit while the remaining two are plain and count single. As you can see the darts total triple, triple, single, single, or a total of eight, just as in Razzle.

The same fast-count system is employed by the Agent, and the results are always the same for the eager player. The player is always fast-counted to a good number until he needs one to win, and then the numbers are counted correctly, so he can never win.

Another form of this dart game is played with six darts that count for what they hit. A total of six or thirty-six is an automatic winner. The only problem is that there are usually just six ones and six sixes on the dart board with the same rule that a dart striking a line counts as three.

Again the fast-count is used along with some kind of conversion system to build the player to a certain score.

BAFFLE BLOCKS: This is called Baffle Blocks because the operator can "baffle" the player with the count.

The game consists of 8 six-sided blocks with each side bearing a number from one to six. Sound familiar?

The blocks are set up toward the back of a board approximately two to three feet from the player. The player spills the blocks over by either rolling a ball or swinging a bat suspended from a chain. Once again the Agent fast-counts the total of the numbers lying face up.

CHIP BOARD: An alley approximately five feet long and three feet wide runs from the front of the game counter to an inside counter. To the rear of this alley is a section once again containing numbered squares, and (you guessed it) the numbers once again run from one through six.

The player spills eight miniature footballs into the squares, and once again the same fast-count technique is used by the Agent.

PEEK STORES

These are Flat Stores in which, unlike the fast-count stores, the Agent employs a technique of mis-calling numbers or hiding them (peeking) from the player.

A common Peek Store is referred to as a PIN STORE. The idea is that the player either tosses rubber jar lids around or points a stick at one of many clothes pins lined in rows inside the booth.

Behind each pin is a number which corresponds to a conversion chart for their worth. (These numbers are concealed to the player.)

If the player rings a pin with the number 140 behind it, it is worth nothing, but a pin with the number 40 is worth 50 yards.

Therefore, if the Agent wants to "help" the player he merely mis-calls the legitimate number when he pulls it off the rack or puts his finger over part of it (see diagram).

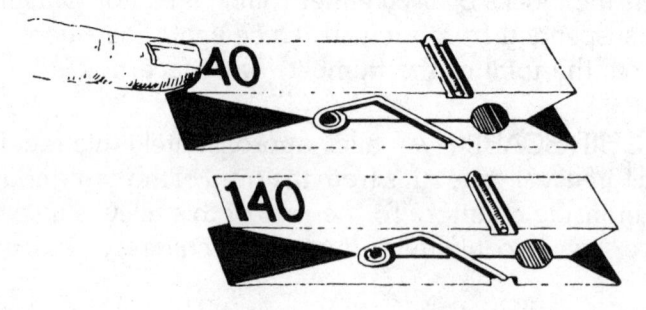

PIN STORE/CHEWING GUM/MATCH BOX: The only difference in these three games is the object used to conceal the hidden numbers from the player. The mis-call and "peeking" of the numbers are the same. Just remember that whether it is with clothes pins, packs of chewing gum or boxes of matches, the player is almost assured of receiving whatever points are needed for half the game on the free try. But the end result will still be the player coming up one point shy at the end.

Another convenient thing about a Peek Store is that the Agent, when challenged, can take just about any concealed number off the rack at random and turn the bad numbers into instant winners by merely concealing part of the number.

BLOWER: Although some of these games are worked as a Hanky Pank, the majority are Peek Stores. The player scooping out one of the ping-pong balls being blown in the air will usually find himself the victim of the same mis-call and peek fraud.

DEVIL'S BLOWING ALLEY: Large rubber balls are recycled down a ramp in front of the players and the same idea as the Blower is used. The player picks one out, hands it to the Agent and once again the Agent either mis-calls or peeks what he wants, at his option.

ABC BALLOON: A game very similar to a Hanky Pank Tag Balloon. Here the player throws darts at balloons. Behind the balloons are tags, each of which has hidden letters or numbers.

In order for the player to win he must accumulate a series of letters or numbers (example: A, B, C, D, E; or 1, 2, 3, 4, 5, 6, 7, 8, 9).

The player is built up just as in RAZZLE by hitting tags calling for H.P.'s, bonuses, etc.

The problem with winning this game is that a certain number or letter needed to win is excluded from the board. It is safe in the operator's apron, but ready to be palmed when needed.

WHEELS: This deadly Flat Store is commonly referred to as a SKILLO or SKILLET. It is one of the few games that depends largely on an outside man to help in the fleecing. This man pretends to be a big winner who is no longer allowed to play, so he entices the potential customer into going fifty-fifty with him. Of course the accomplice has nothing to lose, but the Mark does. The arrow spinning around the board can be stopped at will by a brake located either under the counter or outside the booth (operated by the outside man).

The player is enticed to continue not by a conversion chart but by the odds being reduced by the Agent. In other words, the board is broken down into sections. The only thing wrong is that before the player even comes close to a good section the ante has been doubled to 99 yards.

BEHIND THE SCENES

So now you've seen some of the things that make up a carnival – exciting rides, challenging games and fast-talking Agents. But I've only hinted at what makes the carnival industry such a big business: money.

To get that green into their pockets a lot of people work together (sometimes not so harmoniously). Let's take a behind-the-scenes look at how a carnival comes to your town.

First of all, Carnies know pretty much what is happening about carnivals across the country, and we learn through *AMUSEMENT BUSINESS* magazine. This publication is *The Los Angeles Times* of the carnival industry, keeping the Carny abreast of the latest news, births, deaths, gossip, and a complete section of classified ads. (When a Carny dies it is announced in the AB under "Final Curtain.")

The AB can be found in many bookstores and most public libraries. It would be very helpful for you to obtain a copy during the week prior to visiting a carnival, for many times, after the slang is interpreted, it will reveal what type of operator you can expect to see in action. (Example: if the particular carnival is advertising for AGENTS, ALIBIS, or FLAT STORES, you should be extremely careful during the visit, for these terms are associated with rigged games!) Many ads in the AB tell you to contact the show through the local police department in the town where it is playing. Why are the local authorities so cooperative in acting as a messenger service?... Read on!

Even before a carnival opens, much has already happened. Because carnivals are plentiful, the competition is fierce among them to get a bigger share of the thousands of potential engagements. In order to book an engagement, the carnival owner bids for the particular site through the sponsoring committee.

I am a firm believer in the three-bid system with the results being made public after the awarding of the contract. Such a system would greatly reduce the under-the-table practices which sometimes determine which carnival is extended the privilege of playing an engagement. This can best be summed up by the remark of a carnival owner. "It's getting to the point that the envelope slid under the table has more in it than I get!" Not all committees are on the take, but I've seen enough to know that it is a major problem.

After a date is booked, the ADVANCE MAN swings into action. This employee holds the responsibility of going ahead of the show to arrange for such things as the location, business license, advertising, etc. He puts up the "paper," which means all the posters advertising the arrival of the carnival. If possible a sponsor is sought out, such as the Jaycees or American Legion, for such a prominent group can usually be talked into furnishing the above necessities for a percentage of the carnival take. Such an arrangement is even more important for a show carrying rigged games, because with a prominent sponsor not only endorsing the activities but also having a vested interest in the gross, the chances of a disgruntled Chief of Police or Sheriff sticking his nose in is greatly reduced. The Advance Man has to possess a high degree of salesmanship because his spiel in selling a sponsor can sometimes mean the difference between a mediocre profit and a healthy one. If he can convince the sponsor to take care of the bulk of the advertising, the carnival is already far ahead of the game. Sometimes, when the need arises, it is also the Advance Man's job to pay off a local Chief of Police or Sheriff to allow the carnival's rigged games to operate, but this is usually the Fixer's job.

I don't mean to imply that all carnivals are "racket shows," – ones with lots of rigged games and where gambling is encouraged. Far from it! Many are "Sunday School shows," clean carnival operations.

But let's take a look at the FIXER, or PATCH, of a Racket Show. His primary duties are to fix the local cops and to hold as much of a player's losses as he can when a customer realizes he's been had. The job of a Fixer takes a special breed, for not many people will walk into a lawman's office and offer him a bribe. Of course he does it in a way to make it appear as a donation for the officer's favorite charity, but both the Fixer and the one being fixed know what the "charity" is.

A typical conversation between a Fixer and let's say a small town Sheriff will sound something like this. "I'm with a little carnival that will be here next week, and we'll need a couple of your men to work off-duty security. Now we have some games that are tough, but we don't play to no kids. If a player feels he's been cheated you tell your man to bring him to me, and I will personally take care of the problem. By the way, Sheriff, I'd like to donate this five hundred to your favorite charity." If the lawman takes the money the Fixer knows the rigged games will work with no problem, but if the Sheriff refuses, he knows either to bring in only legitimate games or to by-pass the town. But even if the Sheriff wants to nail the briber he is unable to because the Fixer has been smart enough to cover himself with the pretense of a "donation."

The trait of a good Fixer is also measured by his negotiations with a disgruntled player. His job is to retain as much of the losings for the Agent as possible. He may verbally blast the Agent to make the player feel better or even pretend to fire him, but this is all just an act.

A good Skin Show is a real attraction at a Racket Carnival, for the better the Fix, the wilder the show, often including complete nudity and a little body contact as the girls hover at the edge of the stage. It is also an important ally for a Fixer when he needs to entertain a committee member, police officer, or a disgruntled player.

If the Fixer is unable to reach an "understanding," the carnival operators may still choose to work rigged games without a fix. This is called operating "under the blue." Depending on his arrangement, the Fixer issues orders – the rules that a Fixer gives an Agent by which to work. If the spot is "fixed," the orders are to BAT AWAY, but if not, the Agents are told to take a little and leave a little.

The only time the order to Bat Away is given is when the police have been paid off. I remember working under such orders and watching dumbfounded as the Agent next to me jumped over the counter and directed his player's attention to the Ferris Wheel nearby. With the sincerity of a Baptist Preacher he convinced the gullible player that he must be the luckiest man in the world because the player not only would get five hundred bucks, a color t.v., a stereo, and a half dozen stuffed animals but would get the Ferris Wheel as well! The Agent was so convincing that when the player finally stumbled off with the two small consolation prizes for his twelve hundred dollar loss HE ACTUALLY LOOKED RELIEVED! His biggest concern had been how the hell he would have gotten the Ferris Wheel home if he had won it! I know it sounds unbelievable, but it really happened. The point is that when the orders are to Bat Away, an Agent can offer the player the whole show. Then when the guy's last dollar is in the Agent's moneybox, the Agent can rest easy when he springs his alibi and tells the sucker to take a hike.

The actual setting up of a carnival is a big operation. The rides have to be set up, of course, and their operation and maintenance is performed by ride men called "jocks" or "monkeys." The ride man is considered by many

Carnies to be the lowest position on a carnival Midway. (But I should say that in the Carny social structure, the GEEK is usually the lowest rung of the ladder.) Most ride men make below standard wages, sleep in trucks, and seldom have facilities to bathe, but they still hold a reputation for being ladies' men. I've seen some beauties crawling from the belly of a ride truck, which has prompted a joke among Agents that women must be attracted to the smell of grease.

Rides are a lot safer on the larger shows, not only because of the better pay (which attracts better help) but also because these shows have a superintendent who oversees the RIDE MONKEYS. So the smaller the carnival, the more dangerous the rides may be. Without supervision, an overworked and underpaid RIDE MONKEY is more apt to cut corners. After all, what's a lost cotter key here and there?

The COOKHOUSE also has to be set up. This is the place (although it caters to the carnival visitor) that's mostly for the Carny, giving him discounted meals. The ride help usually gets credit here. The majority of CookHouses are far from clean, and for that reason, I was told my first year to seek out "food stands run by the local sponsor, or committee." After viewing open food subjected to insects and dirt, coupled with the kind of help usually associated with a Cookhouse, I deemed this advice sound. Most of these employees are so underpaid that even the thought of a motel room with bathing facilities is out of the question. Such a worker is understandably less than enthusiastic about his job. After all, the hours are long, the pay is peanuts, and the breaks are so short that if a worker fails to take time to wash his hands after a quick trip to the bathroom, well....

Another problem with some Cookhouses is that the

owner is a Carny. He could care less if the food is rewarmed day after day. I knew a Cookhouse owner who had a chimp and many nights the animal was left inside – so you can imagine the cleanliness of that operation.

Somewhat like the Cookhouse is the G-TOP – a tent or trailer which caters exclusively to Carnies. Regardless of the local ordinance, a Carny can drink and gamble in this private club because the only outsiders invited in are friendly guests such as a sponsor or local lawman. The owner of the portable crap game passes the carnival owner a percentage of what he brings in for the right to operate.

Then the electrical power for the carnival needs to be provided. The JUICE MAN, or the electrician, is a very important employee. Without the Juice Man the engagement could not run smoothly. If you've ever been on a Midway when power was lost you probably shrugged it off as a temporary inconvenience. But to a Carny time is money, and during the down time the Juice Man is the star performer. He is usually paid by collecting so much from each operator for the "cut in," or initial electrical hook-ups as needed.

But the most important figure of all is the CONCESSION MANAGER. He is the man in charge of all concessions on a Mdway. This is an important title; his authority is overridden only by the carnival owner. Among his duties are saying what concessions are booked, determining what locations are given, acquiring off-duty police security, and resolving any complaints arising from the concessions. This is a very profitable and respected position because the pay is usually half of the ten percent collected from the games. Thus a Concession Manager on a major carnival can become quite wealthy in a few short years.

Although the duties are basically the same, a Concession Manager is not to be confused with a "Fixer" or "Patch." A Concession Manager takes care of business in an aboveboard manner, while the Fixer relies more on his expertise in bribing local authorities to look the other way when a customer complains of being ripped off.

MONEY
MONEY
MONEY

An INDEPENDENT OPERATOR is a Carny who owns his own equipment, booking it on various carnival Midways. Most concessions found on a Midway are independent, except for FLAT STORES, which are usually owned by the FIXER or carnival owner. "X" is when an operator purchases the rights to a game, ride, etc. on a Midway. And FENCE TO FENCE is when a carnival controls the entire activities at an engagement. Independence means having to pay whatever price the carnival owner demands for space, but on the other hand, the Concession Manager can control the activities that occur at all the games.

Concessionaires must pay POINTS to the carnival office. This is a percentage of the gross paid for the right to operate on the Midway. When Points are demanded by a carnival owner, it is little more than extortion, but the Independent has little choice. Either he pays, or he goes elsewhere. Since most owners have followed suit with this policy, there is really but one option for the operator; he pays. The Points collected are usually split between the carnival owner and the Concession Manager. To the owner it is unaccountable pocket money, but many times it means a salary to a Fixer, who gets part of the owner's take.

Besides Points, a Carny has other expenses as well. ("Nut" is our term for the expenses of a Carny.) Basic costs are called DINGS, such as for electricity, trash pick-up, etc. These are legitimate, but more and more, the poor concessionaire finds himself faced with paying, paying, paying – such Dings are in no way attributed to the ten percent or "Fix" money!

Then there is PRIVILEGE – the rent a Carny pays in order to operate. A carnival owner charges a concessionaire so much per frontal foot of rent. This FOOTAGE can vary in price depending on the engagement, rising to a hundred dollars a foot. If a concessionaire books five games that total sixty-five feet, he might owe the carnival owner as much as sixty-five hundred dollars, not including the Dings, ten percent, fix money, etc. Some carnival owners charge concessions the same Privilege as rides, side shows, and eating stands, and that is a percentage of the gross. An independent ride owner sometimes is charged more than fifty percent and the only thing furnished by the carnival owner is ride tickets! When the Privilege for games is priced on percentage, the common rate is twenty-five percent for legitimate games and fifty percent for rigged games.

Finally, especially at Racket Shows, there is PATCH MONEY. Each Agent working a rigged game pays the Fixer so much a night to assure his right to practice the trade without worry of being arrested. The amount an Agent pays depends on how much the Fixer needs for this assurance plus, of course, his percentage. I have paid as little as three dollars a night and as much as fifty.

All of this means that there is a lot of money changing hands – and I don't mean just from the Mark to the Agent. That's why I can't understand the myth that the carnival industry is a "nickle and dime" operation. Of course, this myth is beneficial to the carnival industry generally, and is perpetuated by the fact that only a small portion of the actual revenues are ever accounted for. Although the incentive to beat the Internal Revenue Service is quite appealing it presents a rather difficult problem, what to do with the large sums of cash compiled during the season. A bank account is out of the question, because banks keep records. Carrying sometimes thousands of dollars nightly presents an even bigger problem. The most common solution is to purchase traveler's checks, called ABA's. To thwart the determination of the Agent's actual income, he buys the ABA's under a phony name by using the always available fake driver's license.

To answer the question, "Is it true that carnivals are nickle and dime operations?" I'll give you the same answer I offered a congressional aide on one of my seventeen trips to Washington, D.C. (six by hitch-hiking) while trying to generate congressional interest in investigating the carnival industry; "If you believe the carnival industry is an unimportant nickle and dime operation then you also believe in Peter Pan." It is an impossible task to determine just how many "nickles and dimes" change hands among all carnivals. Certainly the Carnies aren't going to volunteer such information; if they did, a great number would be in the federal penitentiary along with other tax evaders. For only a fraction of total monies passing through the carnival industry is ever reported for taxes. Think I'm kidding? Honestly, how many receipts have you ever received on a carnival Midway to substantiate the amount you spent? I can tell you right fast that the answer is none. Oh, you might get a torn ticket from a ride, but that's it.

The truth is, the subject of revenue is the most sensitive of all areas to any Carny, whether it be an Agent, a Concession Owner, Fixer, or Carnival Owner. Perhaps the only carnival workers who aren't secretive about money is the majority of ride help, and that's only because most of those folks are so underpaid that it doesn't matter. But you better believe it mattered to one carnival company when it was raided a few years back by Canadian Officials. Although by last account many of the cases were still pending, according to some Canadian sources, the civil tax penalties were quite substantial. And then there was the Concession Manager for another company who was apprehended not long ago crossing into his native Canada with tens of thousnds of dollars which he had forgotten to mention to the IRS. He was convicted, fined, and placed on probation with other civil cases still pending. The Judge, though quite lenient, couldn't believe the case he had just heard. Well, Judge, all I can say is that those tens of thousands were peanuts compared to the monies unreported each year from the combined carnival industry. And to add insult to injury, many Carnies who have stashed away ten or fifteen grand to lounge the winter months away actually apply for assistance and food stamps. Many others just stash it away, except for the jaunt around the Fair Conventions. I guarantee that if you ever visit one of these Conventions, the enormous amounts of cash being flaunted so freely will make you think you're at a meeting of Arabian and Texas oil men.

I've said that a good Agent could clear around twenty-five hundred dollars at a State Fair. Well, I have played some of these fairs with well over a hundred such Agents. And if they all made what I did, we're talking about a quarter of a million dollars. And that's just the share of a hundred Agents at one ten-day fair! Still think carnivals are nickle and dime? As one carnival owner boasted to me not long ago, "Nobody counts my money but me." Indeed.

I can mention two other instances in which outsiders were astounded at the amounts of cash "lying around" in a carnival office. In Oklahoma and Washington, D.C., carnival companies were raided, and in both cases the officers couldn't believe that more than a hundred thousand dollars was lugged from each safe. And that was from smaller carnival units, playing a low-attendance engagement at the beginning of the season. Can you imagine what would be taken from the office of a major-sized carnival at a state fair?

And just how many "nickels and dimes" are accumulated each year? According to more than one carnival spokesman, the combined annual revenues from all carnivals does not exceed one billion dollars. My question is simply how do they know? I mean, they can't even tell me how many carnival companies there are, how many engagements are played, or how much the carnival owner makes. There is the assessment offered by a so-called "carnival expert" that the average expenditure for each man, woman, and child visiting a carnival is ten to fifteen dollars.

As far as attendance is concerned, just the top one hundred fairs draw fifty-four million people. So take the lower of the two figures (ten dollars per visitor), that comes to over half a billion dollars. And remember, that's just the top one hundred.

Then there is the estimate by the world renowned gambling expert, John Scarne. According to his survey in the early 1960's, he guessed that approximately ten billion dollars a year was spent on carnival games alone. And you should consider the fact that his survey was done some twenty years ago when the price of playing such games was much lower than it is today, and that it did not include any of the money spent on rides, food, side shows, and straight sales.

So who do you believe? I certainly don't know. But just remember what I said about Peter Pan!

Since I began my campaign to expose the bad side of carnival life I have talked about all of these problems. Certainly the "fixing" of local officials is an important one. For years I was a Fixer myself, and the amazing thing is how receptive, and cheap, some public officials are. In Atlanta, in order to operate a carnival around the various shopping centers the cost was a hundred bucks per night, divided between two vice officers. In Corbin, Kentucky, the bribe was about two hundred dollars in assorted kitchen appliances and stuffed animals. In Louisville, Kentucky, while playing a state fair, the cost of three State Troopers "being friendly" was a carload of stuffed animals. Yes, "friendly officials" can be had for simple carnival prizes, as the famous "Canadian Report" will attest. During a raid by Canadian Law Enforcement officers on an American-based carnival, some ninety pages of records were seized showing "gratuity" given to public officials including police officers, sheriffs, chiefs of police, judges, state attorneys, etc. The gifts ranged from cigars, to various expensive gifts, to money. (I "obtained" a copy of this report from the FBI office in Oklahoma City, but to my amazement its implications were never pursued by the Justice Department!)

Such bribes are not always "nickle and dime." In Texas a sheriff is currently serving time for accepting bribes in the thousands of dollars from a carnival to "look the other way" while rigged games were operating. And in Arizona, the former Manager of the State Fair was convicted for accepting bribes in the tens of thousands of dollars from Carnies seeking favorable locations for their rides and booths. Yes, corruption is indeed a part of the carnival industry.

The process of bidding for an engagement is another problem. I have always said that contracts should be based on not only the highest bid offered by an owner for a particular engagement but on more important considerations, such as the quality of the carnival operation and the reputation of the bidding carnivals based on past performances. A good example of the recent bidding wars involves two State Fairs at Sedalia, Missouri and Jackson, Mississippi. The committees eventually made the decision to award their contracts solely on what they termed "the most money," (the highest bid won the carnival date). Certainly, money is a consideration, and it is no great secret that most of the fairs throughout the country have for years been deprived of their share. These two bidding confrontations proved that carnival owners are more than capable of paying big sums for an engagement. In the case of the Sedalia Fair, the lowest of the bids, including one by the carnival that had held the contract for years, was for an amount thousands of dollars more than it had been in the recent past. And as for the Jackson Fair, the company which had held the contracts for decades lost out even though its offer was some three times more than it had been in recent years. Once again, I believe that although a Fair Board or Fair Committee is entitled to seek a fair amount of money, money should take a back seat to overall quality of the carnival operation.

As it turns out, the carnival company which was awarded contracts for both Sedalia and Jackson has been responsible for some questionable actions. At least four times, various law enforcement agencies in three different states have found numerous rigged games working "wide open" in Midways operated by the company. In Cheyenne, Wyoming, one carnival game expert assisting local police in the detection of rigged games was quoted as saying, "I have never witnessed such a racket operation." Numerous arrests and the closing of rigged games followed. In one Texas county, the Sheriff was convicted and sentenced for accepting bribes from the company Fixer for allowing Flat Stores to operate. But the greatest charge made against this particular carnival was made in Arizona. Testifying under the promise of immunity from prosecution, the owner himself admitted in federal court to paying thousands of dollars for favorable locations on the Arizona State Fairgrounds.

To make matters worse, in some states the bidding for a state fair is apparently not opened to competitive bidding. In one case I tried unsuccessfully to have a very lucrative state fair engagement presented for open bidding. But the fair manager refused to disclose what the incumbent carnival paid. This fair has been discussed by the media, different law enforcement agencies and Carnies, as having a past reputation for "wide open" operation of rigged games, and the overpricing of concession space to independent Carnies. There is a lot of corruption going on while in search of those big dollars.

To me, there is nothing worse than a Carny ripping off another Carny, and one of the biggest of such rippoffs is over-pricing by carnival owners for independent concession owners to book at the show. There is no way I will argue the point that carnival owners have a big overhead, but then again, there is no way anyone is going to convince me that a carnival owner who pays twenty dollars a frontal foot for concession space from a fair board is right in recharging an independent as much as five times that amount for the right to seek his livelihood. And if that's not bad enough, many carnival owners extort (and that is the only word I can deem appropriate) ten percent of the total gross generated from each concession. In other words, an independent books his game and the total space along the front of the booths comes to a hundred feet; he could wind up paying the carnival owner ten thousand dollars in rent, not including other "extras." The carnival owner also takes a percentage of the total gross of the booth. If each booth averages five hundred dollars a day in total gross, that means the concession owner (based on 8 booths) is paying the carnival owner an additional four hundred a day. If the engagement runs for ten days, that means the carnival owner has collected over fourteen thousands dollars from one of many independent concession owners.

Now, let's look at the independent's side of it. If the weather is perfect for the ten days, and is working with the same daily gross average per booth of five hundred dollars, less ten percent for the carnival owner, at the end of the engagement his total gross would be thirty-six thousand dollars. That figure is quite impressive but when an average of at least fifty percent is deducted for help and lost merchandise, and the rent of ten thousand is deducted, the impressive figure has suddenly diminished to eight thousand. Next comes such deductions as on-the-spot sales tax (which I admit is never close to the legitimate amount the concession owner should pay), personal expenses for such necessities as food and lodging, insurance, expenses to get his equipment both to and away from engagements; so you can see why many independents pray for good weather. A couple of days of rain could mean the difference between a profit and going in the hole. As for the carnival owner, after paying the fair board two thousand dollars for the hundred feet of space, he is left with twelve grand to ease his "overhead." If he has twenty such independents, his take from the concessions is a hefty two hundred and forty thousand bucks! That can ease a lot of overhead, especially when the bulk of such revenues is passed with no receipts – which means no records, which in turn means, "Forget it, Uncle Sam!"

At the smaller carnivals, where the emphasis for profits rests on the abundance of rigged games, the prime locations on the right are usually reserved for the carnival owner or Fixer. Almost always, these games belong to the fixer or owner, but even if they belong to an independent, you can be assured that these two individuals are "cut in on the action." Many a lawman has been told by the carnival owner or Fixer when a problem arises at one of these games, "I had no idea those type of games were operating!" That is totally untrue. You will never see any type of game on a Midway that the owner or Fixer is not aware of, and believe me, if a Flat Store is working, both persons are reaping part of the profits.

The rigged games could be controlled if a police bust was made on the felony charge of fraud instead of the misdemeanor charge of gambling and if the game owner,

Fixer, and carnival owner were arrested along with the Agent. They are all a part of a conspiracy to defraud the public. As a matter of fact, if the whole carnival was closed every time one of these cheating devices was discovered operating, you would soon see such games become extinct. In short, if law officers stressed that "housing fraudulent activities" was grounds for confiscation of the whole carnival, legitimate Midways would soon dominate.

Another concern of mine is the safety of the rides. It might surprise you to know that very few states regulate the number of carnival companies or engagements operating each year, and in fact, very few states even have an official who is qualified to be a carnival regulator. But there are exceptions and I am proud to say that Maryland is one.

During filming for a segment of the *"20/20" News Magazine*, Geraldo Rivera called on the Maryland Ride Inspector to accompany him on a spot-inspection of several carnivals. And his findings? One huge riding device had no brakes. The ride operator had to put the thing in reverse just to slow its speed. The camera caught one close-up of a ride where there was no safety catch that would supposedly hold the rider in his seat. In the rest of his inspections the results were the same. Such deficiencies can only be blamed on human error. That is why in fifteen years I rode such rides fewer than a half-dozen times. Just think about that for a minute.

You can ask any carnival owner his biggest problem each year, and if he's honest, the answer will be a shortage of good ride help. But knowing the business (and I do), I can certainly see why. After all, it takes a special type of indivdual to work for far below the minimum wage, sleep in a ride truck with no bathing facilities, go dirty for long periods of time, and be looked upon by his fellow Carnies as something less than desirable. Such a character can have little pride in himself, much less in his work. The sooner a ride is erected, the sooner a few bucks will be advanced for a cold six-pack of beer. Now don't you think that he might be tempted to cut a corner?

Now don't get me wrong. There are some Carnies who take great pride in their equipment and work very hard at assuring its safety, but there are also those who could care less.

The bottom line is that there is a definite need for both State and Federal involvement to assure the safety of the carnival patron. Don't depend on a sticker on a ride saying that it has been approved by a local "qualified" inspector. There have been instances of such inspectors being a little too "friendly" with the carnival owner, and you know what that means.

THE FIX

Most of the problems surrounding the carnival industry do not have to do with the economy, communication, or legitimate Carnies' lack of concern. What really hurts the business is the continuing victimization of Carnies themselves. That's right! Carnies many times are victimized by their excessive allegiance to the "Code of Silence," by fear of reprisal from fellow Carnies, and in many instances by over-zealous law enforcement officers looking to make a reputation as a "carnival expert." To me, there is little difference between the arrest of a legitimate Carny operating an honest game and the cheating of a welfare recipient on a rigged game. They are both victims and victims have a tendency to complain. The problem is that the majority of such complaints fall on deaf ears!

I started my carnival career in Atlanta, and I remember how "deaf" some police officers can be when a poor person complains of having been ripped off. On many a dirt lot the routine was always the same. A conned player complained, and two uniformed police officers listened diligently before informing the Mark of his options. "Well," the officer would say, "It seems to me that what you've been telling me is that you've been gambling, and gambling is against the law. I guess I'm gonna have to arrest you and the guy running the game." At this point, the officer would get the Mark to the side and offer some private advice. "Listen," he would whisper, " if I make an arrest and you go to jail, you're gonna either have to pay a cash fine or post bond, which is gonna cost you more than half of what you say you lost. Now you know that all the money you lost is gonna be confiscated as gambling evidence, so you can't use that to get out." By now the poor Mark has started to panic at the thought of going to the slammer. "But there is an alternative," the officer would say. "Now I'm not gonna make any promises, but I believe that the guy running the game doesn't want to go to jail any more than you do. I wasn't there, so I don't know if you really spent what you said, but I will do this. You stay here, and let me go see if I can convince the guy to give you back half of what you say you spent. Hell, I might even talk him into giving you a stuffed toy to boot."

Faced with the prospect of jail, nine out of ten Marks will accept the generous help of the officer. Also, the gambling fine could be substantial and he would likely lose all his game money as contraband. So the disgruntled player walks away with half of the money he had lost and a two-dollar teddy bear. What he didn't know is that such a "compromise" is not only well-used but well-rehearsed between the police officers and the carnival Fixer, and furthermore, the cops are paid rather well by the Fixer to play such a role. And to add insult to injury, those two particular cops knew as much about the rigging of the games as the Carny! But even with their expertise, sometimes it didn't quite work out. The cardinal rule is to "keep a complaint on the grounds." If a complaint gets away from the paid-off cops and goes downtown, chances are that the Carny will have problems. (There are a lot of payoffs, but the best carnival Fixer in the world can't fix every cop!)

This happened at one of the engagements in an Atlanta shopping center. When the player showed up in an "outside" police patrol car, I thought that the black officer working for the carnival Fixer was literally going to turn white. It was only after a heap of bargaining (in which incidentally neither off the paid-off officers was involved) that the Mark was given back all his losings plus a couple of stuffed animals. After the Mark left in the patrol car, the above-mentioned officers made this remark to the Fixer: "If a complaint gets off the lot, we can't help you. You're on you're own."

That is the standard practice. During a 1978 Federal

Grand Jury probe into the wrongdoings at the Southeastern Fair in Atlanta, it was learned that every police officer working the grounds had been given the same orders "to bring anyone complaining about the games to the carnival office and under no circumstances to allow a complaint to leave the grounds." But I do not wish to insinuate that these officers were being paid off by the carnival Fixer. They were merely off-duty cops trying to earn a few extra bucks. Once a complaining Mark had been deposited at the carnival office, they had done their job and hence returned to the Midway. It was at the office that the "compromise" was reached between Mark and Carny.

I remember one time in Oklahoma when an "outside" cop stumbled into such a "compromise." The reason for my vivid recollection is that a "friendly" cop and myself were handling the complaint, when the "outsider" came along and arrested me. Of course, I should have been arrested, but I realized the true meaning of "friendship." It happened like this.

During the fall a state fair in Oklahoma is filled with excitement for football, and believe me, Oklahomans love their football. As usual, this sunny Saturday afternoon found me behind the carnival office sipping a beer and watching the afternoon game. Joining me were a couple of game owners, an independent ride owner, a couple of uniformed police officers, the uniformed watch commander, a "friendly detective," and of course, the Fixer. After all, it was his television and booze; he has the job of entertaining our non-Carny friends. Most of us had chipped into a betting pool for this game. It was well into the fourth quarter, and for the first time since the pools started, I had a decent shot at winning the thing (five hundred bucks). Just then, a Carny working for me in the block game rushed up and told me that two Marks had lost $600 and made a complaint against the blocks. To say that

I was annoyed at this interruption was an understatement. But the football game still had about eight or nine minutes to go, so if I hurried I would have time to get back, count down the clock and, more importantly, to collect my winnings. So I tapped the detective on the shoulder and explained that we had a complaint, and we rushed off to the Midway.

At the block game the Agent was leaning against the back counter drinking a beer. We knew that the Agent working the block was a boozer; in this case, he had not been able to resist the temptation of visiting the nearby beer tent. By now he was so loaded he could hardly talk. When I saw this I forgot all about the football pool. All I could think of was how in the hell he had beaten the two Marks out of over six hundred bucks! While the detective listened intently, I started the routine I had used dozens of times. He, too, knew the routine and was about to flash his badge and give the Marks his old "gambling, jail, or half-your-money-back" speech. But this time he didn't have a chance to give his spiel. As a matter of fact, I didn't even finish mine. "What happened?" I yawned nonchalantly to the Marks. "That guy zonked us out of over six hundred bucks!" one of them started. "Wait a minute," I interrupted. "What do you mean by zonked? Do you mean that you won the game and he didn't pay you? Is that what you're trying to say?" "Well, no, he just talked us out of all of our money." I felt like jerking the boozing Agent over the counter, for even booze is no excuse for cleaning out a Mark. He knew that cleaning a customer out leads to a complaint. But instead I turned to the Agent, "How much did they spend?" "Six hundred and thirty bucks," he slurred. "Give me three hundred dollars and two of those teddy bears," I snapped. I turned my attention back to the Marks. "Why didn't you just tell me you had overspent yourselves? Now, I wasn't here and by rights I shouldn't give you anything back. After all, you're both grown men, aren't you? How old are you?" About that time I felt a hand tugging at the back of my belt. "And how old are *you*?" a voice barked. "Let's go!"

Shocked and confused, I turned around. "Who the hell are you?" I asked, as I was led away from the booth. With his free hand this guy pulled out a badge. "I'm a police officer, and you're going to jail. Now let's go!"

I looked at the friendly detective, but from the surprised look on his face, it was apparent that he could offer no help. As the intruder led me toward the police sub-station, I yelled, "Go get Jake." (Of course I was referring to the Fixer.) When we got to the sub-station, I saw in the door the watch commander, with whom I had just been drinking beer and watching football. At the sight of his familiar face I knew that I would not go to jail. I was soon released, and the Marks got half of their losings back (though, I might add, without the customary two teddy bears). There was also a totally frustrated cop who had not been allowed to do his job.

Oh yes, I lost the pool.

I remember an engagement in Kentucky which promised to be a "red one" — a real money maker. Even though another carnival had just pulled out of town, we were told not to worry, for the coal miners were just returning from a lengthy layoff and had plenty of back pay. For this carnival the fix was in so good that the only question about the deputies working the lot wasn't whether they were "friendly," but whether they were sober. Believe me, they took advantage of the free booze offered by the carnival owner. There was apparently a "friendship" between the carnival owner and the local sheriff. A reporter did some investigating and wrote that a payoff had been made in the sheriff's Lincoln. "Not only did it not happen," retorted the sheriff, "but I don't even own a Lincoln." He did admit that the description of the man seen in the Lincoln seemed to fit a deputy sheriff of the county, who happened to own such an automobile. The carnival owner also denied allegation, but he added that another Carny who was in charge of the games (the Fixer) might have made such a payoff. When asked by the reporter over the phone if he would give a sworn statement to that effect, the owner grew belligerent and hung up.

You may draw your own conclusions as to the above, but many a resident was robbed by rigged games, and not one complaining Mark was given a dime back. Kentucky is a good area for rigged games, and many times the payoffs come cheap.

During one particular engagement of a state fair in Kentucky, my uncle and I were working the block game and were quite frustrated by the order passed down that no gambling would be tolerated, nor would any game operator ask a player for more than one dollar per try. We had followed this rule for six days, and we only had four days left of the ten-day run. We figured that if we were to come out of the engagement with a good profit the rules would have to be "eased." So we decided to take a chance that the Troopers might become "friendly" if we offered them some "gratis" stuffed toys. So I called over three of the Troopers who were responsible for enforcing the rules. I asked one of them what his favorite color was, and immediately the trooper pointed to a huge blue dog hanging from the corner of the booth. When the other two made their choices, we knew that our gamble had paid off. We arranged for the Troopers to pull their unmarked cruiser behind the game after we closed. That night they helped us break into a warehouse as we filled their car with as many stuffed animals as it would hold. They were rightly nervous, for as a high-ranking Trooper would later say, "A trooper is not supposed to accept such gifts, but frequently we do." I don't know whether the three troopers knew they were accepting a payoff, but I do know that my investment of a few hundred dollars in merchandise for friendly officers was well worth it.

The next day I had two Marks playing the block game at a dollar a try when I spotted the Troopers nearing the booth. I looked at my uncle as if to say, "It's now or never," and called them over. "Listen, guys," I started, "You don't mind if me and these two guys do a little light gambling, do you?" Although the look on their faces told me that they didn't like the idea, they made sure both players were over twenty-one, shrugged their shoulders and gave the go-ahead. Before the two players left, I had taken them for over a hundred dollars apiece (which was nothing compared to what some of our Marks would lose in the final days of the engagement). By the time we left town, our dollar-a-try game had blossomed into twenty bucks a try. And all this was in front of our new found "friends." Yes, the gamble worked, and we left Kentucky with over five grand each!

It should be obvious by now that there is certainly no shortage of carnival patrons who become victims of a smooth-talking Carny with a rigged game. As the above instances indicate, in many of these illegal activities law officers are involved – either directly (because of payoffs) or indirectly (because police officers don't know how carnival games operate).

IN THE NEWS

But there is another victim: the honest Carny who is harassed, closed down and sometimes arrested because a misinformed law officer doesn't know the difference between a duck pond game and a Flat Store. Some of these officers boast of being "experts" on carnivals. Believe it or not, some of these are FBI agents! The so-called "expertise" of these agents was displayed on at least two separate occasions.

For years, soldiers had been victimized at base carnivals in North Carolina. In the spring of 1981, when the carnival again came to the base, I suspected that the engagement would be no different. By then I had been working for two years to end such ripoffs, and I thought that what was needed was activity on the Federal level leading to congressional hearings. So I informed agents of the gambling division at the FBI Headquarters in Washington about the flagrant fraud occuring at the military installation. I tried to get through twice, but I found that the agents were not interested... that is, until I let them know that the media was going to expose the whole affair, including the fact that I had tried unsuccessfully to get the FBI to act. Suddenly federal agents were flown from Washington to lend their so-called "expertise" in halting the fraud. They raided the carnival, arrested a number of people, confiscated suspected gambling devices, and talked courteously to the media. But in their haste to save face they stumbled right by rigged games that were left untouched and in fact robbed many more soldiers after the interviews were over. At least one of these rigged games was later reported by a North Carolina newspaper. I found this oversight by the federal agents a little confusing, especially since I later learned that the FBI gambling division in Washington was well aware of how the game was rigged.

The other such instance will forever leave a bitter taste

in my mouth. If it was not for the "cowboy" tactics of these FBI "experts," I believe that the number of rigged games operating today would have been greatly diminished, which would in turn would be a tremendous boost in gathering what I needed from the start, the support of legitimate Carnies. But this wasn't to be, and one of these "experts" can be thanked for busting legitimate Carnies in a Maryland raid.

I must admit that the infamous "Military Blunder" made me more than skeptical about investigating another carnival, but after talking to the carnival owner in Maryland, I agreed that it was time for legitimate Carnies to make their stand against these "glory-seeking, headline-hungry, don't-know-what-they're-doing" experts. I had instigated previous raids against this carnival, and the owner had in fact been quoted in a newspaper as saying about me, "They'll find him in a dumpster." And one of the game owners involved wasn't exactly a fan of mine (I had previously testified against him in a Federal tax evasion case that got him jail time, probation, and a hefty fine). Nevertheless, I agreed to fly up to Maryland. There was a distinct possibility that I was being set-up by these unfriendly Carnies, and certainly I had given them an incentive to seek revenge. But I saw an opportunity to work with the many Carnies who had been screaming about the unfair judgement of some law enforcement officers as to the legality of some games, so I thought the trip was worth the gamble.

When I got to the city, two game owners involved in the raid met me at the airport. It was, to say the least, an uneasy experience. But it didn't take long for them to explain the circumstances of the raid. Two FBI experts from the gambling division in Washington had participated, and there just happened to be a television crew on the grounds at the same time. It sounded all too familiar, but this time I welcomed the publicity. You see, a television film doesn't lie. So we headed to the Washington television station, and there it was. The Carnies were telling the truth! The police officer explaining one of the "rigged" games was completely unaware that the board of the game in question could hardly have been rigged to move. After viewing the film carefully, it was my time to be interviewed; and you better believe that I took no time in stating that not only were the games not rigged, but that it was the Carnies who had been the victims. The reporter doing the interview seemed a little confused as to my stand, for after all, I was the famous carnival "game buster" who had previously spoken out at the same station against another carnival in downtown Washington. But here there was a big difference. In the earlier Washington raid, the carnival had deserved its fate; that whole carnival operation had been geared for rigged games, and veteran Agents had been employed to rob every poor person who stumbled by. On the other hand, the Maryland raid was against Carnies who had gone out of their way to operate honest games. Yes, I made it clear; this time I was on the Carnies' side. If the local police, or for that matter the FBI, wanted a fight then I was ready. And my ammunition? 1) I had previously been recognized in a Federal court as an expert on carnival games; 2) I had trained numerous law enforcement officers throughout the country in inspecting carnivals; 3) I had earlier helped the FBI, and had even made a film to be used at the FBI Academy in Quantico, Virginia; 4) I had served as a guest speaker at a seminar attended by these same members of the local police department. Besides, one of these same games had in fact been declared legal by a Federal judge after the military fiasco. The Carnies were just plain right. Thus, the State Prosecutor's Office ordered the release of the carnival games to their owners. But it was only after being threatened with arrest themselves that the police finally released the games. And how heated did the battle get? When I visited the FBI in Washington, a high-ranking member of the Bureau actually inquired if I had threatened one of his Agents in the gambling division. And my response? "If you're asking me if I threatened to kick his rear end, the answer is no; though I'm not saying I wouldn't have liked to. If you're asking me if I threatened to embarrass him in court, the answer is yes, and I intend to." You can fully understand why. Believe me, I would have liked nothing better than to challenge these FBI "experts."

Another such "expert" tormented legitimate Carnies at a state fair in Mississippi, while at the same time he approved rigged games. Talk about a foul up! He actually gave the green light for rigged "Flukey Ball" games to operate. State Police Lieutenant or not, he needs to go back to "learning" instead of "teaching"!

In 1981, the same carnival company was the target of two police raids within a sixty day period. These events were featured in a "*20/20 News Magazine*" segment shortly afterward. Then yet another carnival was raided in one of the most impoverished sections of downtown Washington, D.C. Rigged games were discovered. Not only were two of the principals of the carnival companies well aware of the illegal acts, but both were ranking officials of the OABA.

"He's a damn liar, and crazy, too," exclaimed William Collins, the Washington lobbyist for the carnival industry, when asked by *The Washington Post* to comment on the raid and my involvement (for I had informed the authorities). What he failed to mention is that every case involving the raided carnivals ended in a conviction, except the one in which the Carny skipped bond. In fact, only one Carny was tried – the rest entered a plea of no contest.

Thus on two occasions an OABA president had been the subject of illegal activities involving rigged games which both the FBI and the carnival trade paper described as nothing short of robbery. These events provided the foundation for the allegations made by CBS. For millions glued to the television set, this Sunday evening broadcast produced a mixture of shock and disbelief, of anger and shame. To the Carny, it was this and more. It was a time of reckoning which forced Carnies everywhere to wonder, "How do you convince your friends and neighbors that we're not all thieves?"

That plea, coming from Hub Luehr, a carnival owner long recognized for being honest, was neither a lone cry, nor was it new. It has been a concern of every legitimate Carny dating back to *The Chicago Tribune's* attack in 1894 that "all Carnies are homeless bums ripping off the public."

Of course, such a general categorization – whether in 1894, 1978, or today – is untrue. It offers a slap in the face to the majority of Carnies doing little more than making a hard, but honest, living as "merchants of entertainment."

Immediately after the CBS attack, the district attorney of Tampa, Florida, told the Carnies gathered at the annual banquet of the Greater Tampa Showmen's Association: "I want people to know how this club annually hosts a Christmas party for 1,200 underprivileged youngsters. They present a fair and a midway and give each child a bag of Christmas gifts worth between $10 and $15. This club is the greatest contributor of all social clubs in this county to the blood bank and cancer fund. You bring laughter and smiles, good cheer and happiness that knows no racial boundaries. You changed the world's subject from sadness to laughter. You've stood up and cheered for America. Without the laughter you provide, the chance to offer an escape from reality, the rides, the music, the entertainment and brilliant colors you provide, this nation wouldn't be what it is. You have done so much to improve the quality of life in America."

Then on the night after "*60 Minutes*," Carnies who gathered at the annual banquet of the International Independent Showmen's Association in Gibsonton, Florida, heard similar accolades from U.S. Senator Richard Stone. "I see it was your turn on television last night. But I would like to let you know when it comes time for people to rally to your aid, all the people to whom you have brought so much joy and laughter will be on your side, as I will."

The key to both addresses was the words: *joy*, *laughter*, and *happiness* – for each is an important purpose of the carnival industry. What is more, the industry makes great contributions to charitable causes. Mr. Salines, the District Attorney of Tampa, spoke of the tremendous contributions of the Carnies in his area, and, without hesitation, Senator Stone could have done the same. The fact is, there are numerous carnival clubs and organizations scattered throughout North America, and each contributes enormous amounts of time and money to a variety of worthy causes.

One such organization, the Showmen's League of America, contributes tens of thousands of dollars each year to a fund that finances the college educations of young people in need of assistance. And these kids need not be Carny kids, nor do the countless thousands remembered at Christmas. But the "helping hand" goes much further. Each year, millions of dollars are raised by charitable organizations through the sponsorship of a carnival engagement. Many a wheelchair, set of crutches, and medical research contribution can be traced either directly, or indirectly, from the proceeds derived from carnivals.

But the most important words come from Hub Luehr:

> "We run a clean operation and I don't think the OABA should or can condone a double standard. There is no room in this industry for crooks."

Carnies have a right to be proud of their heritage, and an even stronger right to disassociate themselves from the "stigma" of their trade. Unfortunately, there is no "Otto Schmidt" to lead them.

It is time for a Carny to step forward and to make a sincere effort to organize the multitude of legitimate Carnies, instead of just talking about what needs to be done. More importantly, we need to stop denying what we know to be the truth. Only then will the real Carnival World flourish, and the victims, both outsiders and Marks, will be things of the past.

On February 12, 1978, a sixteen minute film aired by the CBS "*60 Minutes*" News Magazine attacked the carnival industry making horrid accusations of widespread fraud and corruption "lurking behind the innocent front of a merry-go-round." By no means was the concept new, but because of the age of electronics and the power of television this controversial broadcast was by far the most damaging sixteen minutes in the history of the carnival industry.

CBS asked tough questions about the largest carnival trade organization, the Outdoor Amusement Business Association (OABA), the validity of its Code of Ethics, and the efforts of the organization and its members to "clean up" the carnival industry. Television interviewers implied that those efforts were a sham since many of the OABA members regularly took part in the illegalities being "cleaned up." Four such members were singled out, including Al Kunz, then President of the OABA, and his carnival company, Century 21 Shows.

The CBS allegations prompted a strong response from the carnival trade organization. Rolly Larson, Executive Director of the OABA, commented, "We knew that they (CBS) were going to play up the ripoff idea, just as they do in most of their broadcasts. Personally, I am proud of Al Kunz's performance. Also, I am proud of OABA for the good it does the people it serves. Unfortunately, false charges were made against OABA and some of its directors." "As for illegal games," Larson continued, "OABA categorically opposes them. We support only legal activities. We continually promote our Code of Ethics. Every member signs it, and we cooperate for the good of the industry. All a fair manager, sheriff, or chief of police has to do is close up the illegal games. No doubt illegal games still exist, but where they exist it is as much a fault of crooked politicians and sponsors as it is of the game operators. Rather than blame OABA, which is trying to clean up the industry, they should look to themselves and clean up City Hall, then there wouldn't be any crooked games."

During this time at least one other OABA spokesman charged that fraudulent games existed and operated for the most part because of the willful participation of corrupt officials. And there had been earlier defenses of the OABA, too. During an interview appearing in the September 5, 1977, edition of *U.S. News & World Report*, OABA President Al Kunz stated, "this used to be a pretty rough business, but it has really cleaned up. Now our trade association (OABA) has a tough Code of Ethics, and we stick by it and protect our customers."

U.S. News printed the story under the headline, "CLEANED-UP CARNIVALS TAKE OVER THE MIDWAYS." From its appearance Mr. Kunz and his carnival company might seem to have been cleared. But what Mr. Kunz failed to mention during the *U.S. News* interview and what Mr. Larson omitted after the "*60 Minutes*" broadcast, was the following:

> In August of 1976, a total of sixteen carnival employees were arrested for fraud and gambling on the "Century 21 Shows" Midway in Minnesota. Thousands of dollars, several "Razzle Dazzle" (rigged) games, and some business records were among items seized. One police official said that some players had lost as much as $250 on the games, and some of the television sets offered as game prizes were empty shells.
>
> In Atlanta during April, 1977, a raid by members of the county solicitor's office led to the arrest of three carnival employees of the "Century 21 Shows" and the seizure of another "Razzle Dazzle" game. (I should note that the arrests were for gambling, and not for fraud involved with the Razzle.) The lawmen's interest had been stirred by a front-page story in the local paper describing in detail how numerous game players had been "taken." Each of the victims had been poor blacks of the impoverished section of Atlanta, and each had apparently spent what few extra dollars he had from his monthly welfare check.

It should be pointed out that "Razzle Dazzle" games fall into a category of carnival games that offer a player absolutely no chance of winning. Also called "Flat Stores" (because the Carny operator can "flat out rob a player"), the odds of winning are so minimal that a gambling expert for the FBI estimated that, in order to win, a player would have to spend as many dollar bills as would encircle the earth at its widest point to a depth of three feet when stretched end to end! And the carnival trade paper, *Amusement Business* magazine, was just as critical in its description of the game when it asked, "Does anyone believe a Razzle was ever considered legal in Canada or anywhere else?" Not if bank robbing isn't.

Since the "*60 Minutes*" show, there have been other news stories which ignore the existence of legitimate, honest Carnies and group them with fraudulent operators. In a June, 1979, expose by Brian Ross of NBC News, the target once again was the "Century 21 Shows" and the operation of Flat Store games. But this time legitimate Carnies had to bite the bullet a little harder for not only were they again being associated with fraud but with the robbing of kids as well. After Ross showed the operation of a Flat Store game, a hidden camera showed two youngsters playing it and being cheated. And what was done by legitimate Carnies to curb such problems with the industry? Nothing!